KNIGHTS *of the* TELE·ROUND TABLE

Knights

of the

TELE·ROUND TABLE

3rd Millennium Leadership

Insights for *every* executive—especially those who must manage from afar

JACLYN KOSTNER, Ph.D.

WARNER BOOKS

A Time Warner Company

This Warner Books edition is published by arrangement with the author.

Warner Books, Inc., 1271 Avenue of the Americas, New York, NY 10020

 A Time Warner Company

Printed in the United States of America

First Warner Books Printing: September 1994

10 9 8 7 6 5 4 3 2 1

Library of Congress Cataloging-in-Publication Data

Kostner, Jaclyn
    Knights of the tele-round table : 3rd millennium leadership insights for
every executive, especially those who must manage from afar / Jaclyn Kostner.
        p. cm.
    ISBN 0-446-51879-4
    1. Work groups. 2. Communication in management. 3. Leadership.
    4. Management—Fiction. I. Title.
HD66.K68   1994
658.4' 036—dc20   94-14841
                                                                    CIP

Book design by H. Roberts

To Jim and Jim, Jr.

Contents

Acknowledgments ix

Introduction 1

The Coin 5

The Contact 13

Excalibur 25

The Round Table 43

The Joust 65

Camelot 81

Lancelot 99

Merlin 125

The Fall 147

The Gift 161

ARTHUR'S INSIGHTS *169*

THE EXCALIBUR AWARD *175*

ABOUT JACLYN KOSTNER, PH.D. *179*

Acknowledgments

For all of the superb and supportive friends, relatives, clients, professional associates, and others who have helped me along with this book, this is my chance to say thank you.

To Jim Kutsko, Sr., who created the wonderful title *Knights of the Tele-Round Table,* and the fabulous last sentence. Your brilliant mind is like Lancelot's and your character is like Arthur's! Throughout the evolution of the book, your constant feedback on the story line, especially from the male perspective, helped me make the characters real. Your genuine excitement about the story as it evolved helped me know I was on the right track. Your encouragement and support were wonderful and very important to me.

To Dr. Judith Briles, who has been not only a special friend, but also an incredible mentor and role model.

Thank you for connecting me with your network and opening doors that otherwise might have been closed.

To Dr. Carl Larson, my esteemed professor and guide during my doctoral work at DU. Your fabulous research on high performance teamwork launched me into this exciting field. I am grateful for your friendship and support.

To Robert Kriegel and Brian Tracy, respected and well-known authors who supported this book without knowing me personally. In your busy and successful careers you managed to find the time to extend a helping hand to a new business author. I am honored by your kindness.

To Peggy Sagan, whose excellence in leading a dispersed team of authors, editors, and marketing experts on my first major book ten years ago sparked my interest in leadership across distance. You are a role model for women and all distributed leaders. You changed my life!

To George Davis, Tom Schlegel, and Robert Vicek for sharing your wisdom, perspectives, and exceptional insight over the last several years. The discussions I have had with each of you about business and leadership have been intriguing. I am overjoyed with your reaction to the book!

To Jamie Raab, my editor, whose cheerful support and unbridled enthusiasm for this book seem boundless. Thank you for welcoming me so warmly into the Warner family. It is a joy to work with you and your colleagues at Warner Books.

To all of the additional people that offered to read and review the prepublication version of the book, thank you to Mal Cleland, Jim Decker, Ron Eckhardt, Michael Gianetti, Gail Hytner, Jessica Janovsky, Pat Keller, Suzanne

Acknowledgments

Mulvee, Betty Naglic, Dave Near, Bob Patti, Marquesa Pettway, Gordon Pierce, Sandra Poland, Ken Radziwanowski, Tamara Sheppard, Christy Strbiak, Karen Wainwright and Pat Whitelock, my dear friend, whose superb detailed feedback helped me crystallize my ideas.

To Edward De Croce, whose talent with a camera is unsurpassed. You are the only professional photographer in my life that has taken pictures of me that I like.

To friends and family who listened, encouraged, and otherwise supported this effort: Fran Buys, Judy Gardner, and Vicki Thomas Martin. And to you, Mom, for being so excited about my success. I'm happy, too!

Introduction

*I*magine yourself faced with the greatest leadership challenge of your life—a geographically distributed team that's failing. When one day, in a flash, you are connected across millennia to be personally mentored by the most legendary multi-site leader of all time—King Arthur of Camelot.

In this business novel, you will meet a modern-day project leader, Jim Smith. He faces a modern-day leadership dilemma—*getting results with a team where some members don't report to him or don't work at the same location.*

In an entertaining and engaging manner, Arthur shares his techniques for aligning and engaging the Knights of the Round Table. With all of the wisdom and finesse one would expect from a legendary king, Arthur shows Jim how to bridge the *geographic* distance that separates his knights. King Arthur also shares his technique for bridging the *interpersonal* distance as well, so that, despite distance, the knights can act as one cohesive group.

Arthur's leadership techniques are relevant for Jim Smith, as well as all leaders of distributed work groups, including:

- Alliances with customers, suppliers, and other vendors
- Downsized staffs that must share resources across distance
- Sales or service organizations that span multiple locations
- Cross functional teams where team members don't report to the leader
- Remote manufacturing, internationally shared R&D, or other remote groups
- Strategic partnerships and other virtual organizations
- Telecommuters

In the story, Jim wants to bridge the distance, but doesn't know how to do it. The lessons he learns from King Arthur's experience will engage your mind and change the way you view your role as a remote leader.

As an intellectual overview, King Arthur mentors Jim using key symbols of the legend familiar to us all.

Excalibur. To get high performance, the remote leader's greatest *people* challenge is to develop trust. Remote teams have a uniquely hostile environment in which to develop trust. First, distant team members tend not to know each other well. Second, they have few opportunities to develop trust in the traditional way (at one location).

Third, they tend to communicate poorly with one another across distance, which destroys trust. If these trust issues are ignored, performance will suffer and synergy across distance will never occur.

Only through building high-level trust can a virtual (multi-site) leader expect to get high-performance results. Excalibur, the symbol for leadership, is a reminder of the virtual leader's critical role to develop *trust*.

The Round Table. Groups that work across distance tend not to see themselves as a team or a unified group. Instead, they are more drawn to people and events at the local level. The Round Table reminds the remote leader to create symbols and structures that solidify the unity of the dispersed work group.

The Joust. Virtual work groups tend not to share information as equally or as effectively across distance as is typically needed. One reason why is they lose traditional forums to do that (such as informal meetings at lunch or around the coffee pot). The Joust helps the remote leader identify some ways to solve the problem.

Camelot. Virtual work groups need clear structures to focus effort and energy across distance. Vision, mission, and goals are important for all groups, including those split by distance. Remote teams, however, need something more to align people and performance, despite distance. This chapter introduces the decision tool, which is used to streamline activity from distributed locations into one uniform direction.

Lancelot. In virtual work groups, geographic separation tends to foster relationships with those on-site, while inhibiting them with others off-site. Inequities in those relationships can pit those away from the leader's location against those who are on-site with the leader. Lancelot reminds the virtual leader to attend to the unique needs of the people at distributed locations.

Merlin. With distributed teams, people in each separate location have different information. Equally important, each location also has a different *context* from which they send and receive information. As a result, miscommunication is exacerbated because of the inequities of information and context. Merlin is the symbol for how to communicate more effectively across distance.

This book is written to entertain you, yet alert you to critical success factors to bridge geographic and interpersonal distance. So, sit back and relax. And enjoy the story as each page unfolds the virtual leadership adventure.

Jaclyn Kostner, Ph.D.

The Coin

"No one's *ever* going to believe me," Jim Smith thought to himself. "Why *should* anyone believe me? At first, I didn't believe any of it myself. Everything that happened was so strange I thought I had been dreaming. Now I know I wasn't. It *all really happened*—to me! And it changed my life, forever."

The story began one crisp autumn evening at Heathrow Airport near London. Jim Smith, leader of a geographically distributed team, had just finished a week's business in Europe. He was about to begin his return trip to his office in Atlanta.

Jim lingered patiently in the crowded passenger waiting area until the departure gate for his flight was announced. As soon as the gate number was posted, he began the long walk to his gate. Jim never noticed the heavy crowds of people that suddenly were no longer there as he entered the long concourse to his plane.

A moving sidewalk made the long walk down the seemingly endless concourse seem not quite so long. Jim had always liked the sensation of walking briskly down a moving sidewalk. His rapid pace, combined with the speed of the moving sidewalk, created a light breeze that felt wonderful against his face. Jim had always enjoyed that sensation. In some strange, yet understandable way it made him feel like Superman.

He gazed out the concourse windows at the sunset that was rapidly turning into nightfall. He could hear the low rumble of a jet just taking off in the distance. As he looked once again inside the concourse, he noticed a pay phone ahead. "I had better check my voice mail before I get on the plane," he said to himself.

Jim made the call by credit card. When he hung up, though, strangely, he heard a coin drop into the return slot. Almost instinctively, he reached inside. To his delight, he immediately found a coin.

"That's funny!" he said as he pulled out a strange-shaped, ancient-looking metal coin. It didn't look like any of the other currency Jim had been using in the UK on his business trip there this past week.

Glancing at it briefly, he thought, "Maybe this coin will bring me the luck I need to turn around my world-wide project team! I'm going to almost need a miracle to pull *this* team together." He flipped the coin in the air and caught it. Then he stuck the coin in his pocket, walked to the gate, and finally boarded the flight.

Little did Jim know how the coin would change his life.

Once the flight was airborne, the flight attendant came by. In a voice that reminded Jim of his college sweetheart, she asked, "Would you like a beverage before we serve dinner, Mr. Smith?"

"Yes. Coffee, please . . . uh, Gwen," he responded, as he read her name tag. After criss-crossing the globe, having a poor sleeping schedule, and handling all the stress— he was dragging. He was hoping a jolt from the caffeine would revive him so he could stay awake long enough to watch the in-flight movie.

As she poured the coffee, Jim pulled the old coin out of his pocket. He was intrigued by its strange shape and wanted to take a closer look at it. One side of the coin showed a raised outline of a very simple royal crown. The other side showed some letters. Although some were worn totally away, Jim could read an X, C, A, [some space] and a P or R.

When Gwen handed him the coffee, Jim was still examining the coin that now rested on his open palm.

"That looks like a *very* old and *very* valuable coin," said Gwen. Then, leaning her face closer to his, she said privately, yet firmly, *"I would hold on tight to it, Mr. Smith. Coins like that can have magical powers."* As she cast him a mysterious, all-knowing glance, Jim's hand closed itself around the coin.

"Do you mean the three-wishes thing, like in Aladdin?" Jim said teasingly, expecting her to laugh along with him. "Do you think I can use this coin to wish for a billion dollars or for world peace or something like that?"

But Gwen didn't laugh. Slowly, yet emphatically, she whispered into his ear, "Not three, Mr. Smith. *One.* Not *anything* in the world. *One.* The coin will give you the answer to *one* question you've been asking yourself a lot lately. When you want to know the answer, rub your thumb *once* over the letters. You'll be connected to the answer you seek."

Jim felt like he was an unwilling actor in a sci-fi flick. Who was this woman? Did she have psychic powers? Could she read his mind? Or was she just off the wall?

As her attention was diverted to other passengers, Jim gulped. One question *had* been on his mind a lot lately. *"How do I pull the people on my worldwide project together into one cohesive partnership?"* How did *she* know this one question had been haunting him for the past month?

Jim had been a very successful leader with other projects, where everyone worked under one roof and everyone reported to him. It was easy to monitor the work, identify problems fast, and take spontaneous action.

Jim was not having the same success, though, with his worldwide team. "I feel like I am leading six small teams rather than one cohesive unit," he often lamented to himself. Leading a team with six different sites, five different functions, three different companies, and three overseas locations was the greatest leadership challenge he had ever faced.

Jim knew that leading a distributed team was a whole

new challenge he had to tackle successfully. He knew the key to his success was to learn how to help the team bridge the geographic and interpersonal distance that separated the people.

Jim wished he could find a mentor or coach who had successfully led a high performance partnership across distance. Every other remote leader he knew, however, struggled as Jim did.

While he was thinking, Jim unconsciously brushed his thumb over the letters of the coin. Suddenly, for only a split second in time, a blast of brilliant light filled the cabin. The light was as quick as a flash on a camera, only much brighter. Then, in a nanosecond, all traces of it were gone.

Jim suddenly looked about the cabin. The look on his face clearly asked, "What was that?"

As he gazed at the people around him, though, no one else was reacting at all. They were still talking, reading, or watching the news video. No one appeared startled. And no one else was looking around the cabin questioning the sudden blast of light.

Jim then opened his fist and looked at the coin. He wondered if the coin had something to do with the flash. His more rational side, though, told him that coins have no magic powers. He closed the coin back into his fist.

He looked out the window to see if the flash was from lightning. All Jim could see, though, was complete darkness outside. In the glass, though, a faint reflection caught his eye. Jim noticed an old face with tired, yet sparkling eyes, looking back at him. "God, I look awful!"

he thought to himself, as he quickly took another sip of coffee.

To sharpen the reflection in the window, Jim turned on the reading light above his seat. The image was only slightly clearer. "I need to get my beard trimmed, too," he said as he reached his hand to rub the familiar hairs on his chin.

But his hand didn't find a beard. It found skin! At that second, Jim suddenly realized that something was wrong—*very* wrong! With his heart in his throat, he suddenly remembered: He had shaved his beard last week!

Jim jerked his head back from the window as fast as a snapping turtle protects itself from its worst enemy. What was going on? He looked at the coin in his hand again, and then he quickly closed his fingers over it. Adrenaline was shooting through every limb of his body as Jim tried to comprehend something he *knew* was impossible.

In automatic pilot mode, he walked up the aisle, opened the lavatory door, then closed and locked it. The palms of his clenched fists rested on the edge of the small sink counter. Jim's arms supported his body.

For a few moments, he stood there silently, eyes fixed on his hands. Was he dreaming? "Yes! Absolutely, this must be a dream! I can feel the reality of the floor under my feet, but I *know* this must be a dream!" he said quietly in a somewhat quivering voice.

The hand without the coin threw some water on his face. The cool water felt refreshing on his skin. It made the tingling sensation from sensory overload seem to decline to a more tolerable level. Jim let the water drip off his face to the sink and floor below.

After he had calmed down, Jim made the mistake of looking up at the mirror. Before he could think, his reflexes kicked in again. The image in the mirror wasn't Jim! *It was someone else!*

In an instant, Jim and the image in the mirror each screamed simultaneously. Jim's panic suppressed his scream to a sound barely more audible than a whisper.

Never in the history of mankind did any human exit an airplane lavatory so quickly! With split second speed, Jim was out of there, slamming the door behind him.

Gwen, having just changed an in-flight video tape, saw Jim's almost cartoon-like instant exit. Jim stood trembling in front of the closed door, with all of his might, holding it closed. Like in some horror flick, the back of his body pressed so hard against the door it was as if his might alone would keep the monster inside. Jim's knees were trembling so hard that he knew the slightest force would cause his legs to crumble like fine china dropped onto a marble floor.

With words that sounded like an audio tape on fast forward speed, Jim blurted out, "It's out of order! Don't go in there! Don't let *anyone* go in there!" Jim's expression looked like he had just seen a ghost. He swallowed hard and looked to Gwen for comfort.

"No pro-blem-o!" Gwen said calmly, in a pseudo-Spanish phrase. Gwen's calm voice somehow seemed to reassure Jim he wasn't really crazy. "I'll put a sign up."

That sounded like a great idea to Jim, unaware of how tightly his fist grasped the coin.

Gwen continued, "Here, use this other one. *It's working*," Gwen suggested, pointing to the adjacent lavatory. Jim wasn't expecting that response.

Jim's first inclination was to say "Not on your life! Nada. Nyet. *Not!* You couldn't *pay* me to go in there ever again for the rest of my life!" Something, though, was drawing him in there.

He reluctantly opened the door to the adjacent lavatory ever so slowly. He creeped inside. His heart pounded so loudly he felt everyone on the plane could hear it.

There he stood again, opposite the image he could not seem to escape.

The Contact

Jim closed the door and locked himself inside the airplane lavatory.

"Who *are* you?" gasped Jim, now realizing the male image in the mirror was not his reflection. It was the same image he now knew had looked at him in the window earlier in the flight. In the shock of the moment, Jim's only comfort was that the image seemed to be as surprised and frightened as he.

In the background behind the man in the mirror, Jim could see a grassy meadow clearing, cradled by clusters of beautiful old trees. In the distance, Jim could see silhouettes of several horses grazing lazily. On another part of the field, Jim also saw a small group of people clustered in a circle around a bonfire. The scene seemed calm and peaceful, in such contrast to the tension in the face of the male image that faced Jim.

Jim could hear the crickets singing and the wind gently blowing in the dawn or dusk, Jim couldn't tell which. He could see the glow of the fireflies illuminate the man's distinctive facial features. The picture was so clear and so lifelike that Jim was tempted to reach through the mirror. But his shattered nerves kept his arms, legs, and body absolutely frozen.

The man had a kind face. But his eyes seemed sad and tired, as if he had reached that point in time where he lost everything that was important to him. Those eyes reminded Jim of his friends who got the axe in corporate cutbacks. It reminded Jim of other leaders whose projects failed. It reminded Jim of the way he felt inside when his wife asked for a divorce. The man's expression was one Jim knew well. It reflected a universal sadness that didn't need words to express.

The assistant who had been trimming the man's beard was excused. After the assistant was some distance away, the man slowly responded to Jim's question. "My name is Arthur . . . *King* Arthur." With those words, Arthur gently reached down to his side, picked up his golden crown, and placed it regally on his head.

Jim was surprised by the simplicity of the crown. It was not covered with diamonds and precious stones like the ones Jim had seen displayed at the Tower of London over the weekend. Arthur's crown had no pouf of velvet underneath to highlight the glow of the gemstones. No, instead, Arthur's crown was magnificently simple. In fact, it looked just like the one drawn on the coin.

"King Arthur! . . . *of Camelot?*" Jim said, with a gulp so huge he felt his Adam's apple almost bounce off the floor. Then Jim said to himself, "*King Arthur!* Impossible! King Arthur supposedly lived centuries ago—if he ever lived at all! How can I be talking with someone that's been dead or is only a legend?"

Instantly, Arthur sat up straight, and his chest swelled with pride. "Of course . . . *Camelot!*" replied the mighty King, remembering all the while the magnificence of the Camelot he created and nurtured. The smile on Arthur's face glowed like sunlight, radiating warmth from his heart and soul. His reflections of that moment in the sun held great meaning to him, as it did for all the others that basked in Camelot's warmth.

Lost in the moment of this incredible exchange, Jim was awestruck. Having exchanged only a handful of words with each other, Jim could feel the man's depth of character and conviction. Jim was suddenly almost overpowered by a sense of peace and goodness, just like he felt when he was a small child enjoying stories of the Round Table.

Then Jim said, "Why, *yes!* King Arthur and the Knights of the Round Table is a legend known throughout the world! It was always my favorite story when I was a small child as it was for all of my brothers, sisters, cousins, and friends. Writers have kept your brave deeds alive for over a thousand years!"

On hearing those words, Arthur was filled with *such joy!* He stood tall, and then threw both sides of his warm cape behind his shoulders. In a tone of startled disbelief, he exclaimed, "People know the story *throughout the world*!"

The tears that came to him at that moment made his eyes sparkle. The sadness he showed earlier had vanished, replaced by pure, childlike happiness! Arthur's whole life, his every breath, was committed to creating and living his dream—Camelot. Like all great leaders, he wanted to bequeath that beautiful dream to thrive in history. He wanted the human miracle of Camelot and the Knights of the Round Table to be known throughout the world. And now he knew it was.

Suddenly Arthur's mental dance of joy stopped as fast as a bullet smashing into a brick wall. "Did you say a *thousand* years?" After a few seconds of silence that seemed like an eternity, he forced out a few more words. "From what year do you speak, my friend?"

Jim tried to respond, but the words came out of his mouth at a snail's pace. "We are nearing *the year 2000,* Your Majesty!"

"The year *2000*? You live in the year *2000*? How can that be true?" exclaimed Arthur, in a high pitched, excited voice fueled by his adrenaline-filled body. Suddenly, the king, too, found it difficult to speak. With all of his might, he finally forced out one sentence, one word at a time, "My . . . year . . . is . . . 597!"

Arthur and Jim stood frozen at the reality that had just exploded in front of them. For the first time, both men realized they were somehow connected across time. In an instant, each of their faces reflected a world of emotions all at once. Their disbelief, yet their belief. Their fear, yet their excitement. Their confusion, yet their wonder.

Arthur struggled through his next sentence. "Could it be that we are communicating across over *1400 years of time?*" The king could barely force the words out above a whisper. The thought of a future so distant from his own took his breath away.

The impact was no less dramatic for Jim. In some ways, it was good that Jim couldn't see himself in the mirror, because his jaw was hanging open, in complete and total shock. Jim thought to himself, "At work, I've skipped over time zones with video conference technology. I've eliminated time zones with E-mail and voice mail. But, is it possible I've skipped through some kind of time warp to be able to talk with a royal legend?"

"Fourteen hundred years!" Jim repeated out loud, slowly and almost robotically.

After a moment of silence, the excitement of the encounter temporarily raised Arthur's voice an octave. In a point of childlike discovery, he said, "Merlin *has* to be behind this."

Then, in his normal deep tone, Arthur shouted a message to the heavens. He wanted to say the words loud enough that his precious mentor and friend would hear it. "Oh, thank you, Merlin. What wonderful gifts of experience you bring me just as you did when I was a child!"

Arthur's eyes then looked straight at Jim. The king's curiosity about his legacy suddenly overcame him. Here was someone who could tell Arthur about all that survived him. Here opposite him was a person who could hand

Arthur every answer he sought about the king's future. Eagerly, Arthur asked, "What do you know about Camelot, friend? What has survived the centuries?"

Jim responded, "There is so much to tell, Your Majesty. Nearly everyone knows the legend of you, Sir Lancelot, and Gwynevere. I also know about the fabled Round Table, the Sword Excalibur, and Camelot itself.

"It has been many years since I have read the story, so I don't remember many of the details. I do know that you were an exceptional leader. You were able to get the knights from all over England to change from war to peace. Despite distance and a history of war, you got everyone to band together to create something wonderful throughout all of England."

Arthur was unaware of the sparkle in his eye, as a feeling of relief overcame him. "You know of all of these things! All of these parts of my world survived 1400 years!" said Arthur, as he sat down, ecstatic. The reflection in the mirror showed both men smiling. The smiles acted like anchors, pulling both of them closer together across space and time.

Arthur had a million questions forming in his mind. He began to blurt them out in rapid succession. "Have you visited Camelot in your time, friend? What does it look like? Have you touched the Sword Excalibur? Who is my successor? Does he undo all that took a lifetime to build?"

Arthur was ready to ask many more questions, but the painful look on Jim's face told him to stop. To Jim, every question Arthur shot felt like a bullet in the spirit of the moment. With each question, Jim's expression gradually changed from joy to sadness.

Jim did not want to give Arthur the bad news that there is no trace of Camelot. He didn't want to say that many historians felt that the great King Arthur of the legend never existed. He didn't want to relay that the Sword Excalibur is not with the royal treasures in the Tower of London.

The intensity of the look on the King's face, however, told Jim that a prompt answer to the king's question was imperative. Jim felt compelled to tell his royal friend the truth. And so he did.

The happy spirit inside Arthur instantly vanished, and sadness stood in its place again. How could it be that his reign as king and his beautiful Camelot are not recorded as historical fact? How could Camelot, so alive and important in his day, die into the earth, without a physical trace to the generations that follow?

Arthur sat down. His head and shoulders stooped forward. His face reflected the shock of the unexpected news. King Arthur was to be known forever only as a fable, not as a historically great leader of England. The future did not recognize him as ever having been born to the earth. This knowledge was devastating to Arthur.

"Why is it that life teaches us so many lessons in so many painful ways," the king muttered in a voice barely loud enough for Jim to hear.

After a long pause for his royal brain to process the news, Arthur finally spoke, "I am overwhelmed by this news, my friend. I am old now. I have lived a full life. I have learned so many lessons. The sadness of knowing that Camelot has no life in the year 2000 is tough to bear.

"As I talk with you, I stand on the battlefield outside my castle. While I was away on a hunting trip, rebels took my castle, imprisoned my wife, and expelled my friend Lancelot. I and my loyal knights are just planning what we should do to regain my kingdom.

"Your news gives me an answer I am afraid I don't want to hear. If we are not in history, perhaps this is one battle Camelot and I won't survive."

Both men stood in silence. Jim's mind frantically tried to find words to comfort the king. It was as futile as finding words to comfort his best friend whose mother just died after a long illness. Jim wondered how anyone ever finds words that truly comfort in such a loss.

In a flash, the silence was broken by Arthur himself. "In my life, Merlin taught me that all things happen for a reason, my friend. I do not understand why you and I have connected across the ages. But I do know that this must be an opportunity that you and I are to explore and do something with."

Arthur then blurted three questions, "Tell me, friend, what is your name? Are you a king or a knight in the year 2000? What is that strange place in which you reside?"

Jim had no idea how he was going to explain that he was in a bathroom in an airplane 37,000 feet in the air, somewhere over the Atlantic! For one brief flash, Jim was hoping there wasn't a hidden camera that was recording this conversation for broadcast on *Candid Camera*!

Jim explained, "The first part of your question will be a lot easier to answer than the last . . . Your Majesty."

Jim knew he was about to shock and confuse his royal counterpart. He began to answer the questions, however, as briefly as he could. "My name is Jim, Sire. I am not a king or a knight. I am the leader of a project team that circles the world."

"*Circles* the world? You mean the world is round, not flat!" said Arthur, laughing at the concept. "What is a project team that circles the world?"

"A project team is a name given to a group of people that works together to create a product or deliver a service. I am the leader of the project, but the people who work with me are distant from me. Although we work apart from one another, we have to operate as one team to get the result we seek."

The look on Arthur's face said Jim's explanation went right over his head. Arthur said, "So you are a merchant?"

Wanting to be clearer, Jim tried to relate the concept to Arthur's experience. "Well, Your Majesty, not exactly. Actually, what I do is very much like what you did . . . er, I mean do, Your Majesty. As King, you are the leader. The knights are your team. Your project is Camelot.

"Your knights lived and worked at a distance from you most of the time. Despite distance, though, you brought them together to create Camelot. I, too, am trying to pull the people on my project together to create a Camelot of my own in my time."

Arthur could relate to Jim's revised explanation. "Ah! Now I understand, Jim. So, tell me of your success. Did you create your Camelot yet?" inquired Arthur, eagerly awaiting the good news.

"Actually, I am only beginning the process, Your Majesty. I have led other projects. But the people on those projects worked together, in one location. I thought that leading people distant from me would be no different. But it *is* different, and I am, only now, being able to see the problems.

"It is so tough to lead a project where people are out of sight most of the time. We have such pressure for performance nowadays that I can't risk failure. I don't know what I have to know to be successful," relayed Jim, honestly laying his biggest fear on the table.

Arthur's mind was processing this information with the speed of a computer. After a moment, Arthur blurted out, "That's it! That's the link! *I* know how to lead from a distance! You can learn from *me!*"

Arthur's excitement about the match grew by the second. He continued, "Even now, this dark hour of my life lights up opportunities for growth. We can both learn from my successes and my mistakes as a distant leader, Jim. I can help you, just as Merlin helped me.

"In return for my gift of knowledge, Jim, I will ask you to do a favor for me. I don't know what that favor is yet, but I do know I will ask it of you. Does that sound acceptable to you?"

It all made perfect sense, and Jim could hardly wait to get started. Jim said, "Yes! It does, Your Majesty! We'll create a partnership across the ages to help each other. I can help you and you can help me!"

Suddenly, Arthur's and Jim's attention was interrupted by someone pounding on the door to the lavatory. An unhappy passenger shouted sarcastically through the door, "Hey, buddy, did you die in there? The other bathroom is out of order, you know. And five of us have been waiting!"

In the excitement of the moment, Jim thought, "No, I just started to live!" Then he said to the person outside the door, "Sorry, but I'll be a few more minutes."

Jim then looked at Arthur and said, "Your Majesty, do you remember what you were doing before we connected with one another?"

"While I was having my beard trimmed, I was holding this old coin Merlin gave me when I was a child," responded the royal highness. Arthur held the coin up for Jim to see.

Even in limited light, Jim could easily see the coin's rippled edges. The coin looked just like the one that Jim found in the phone booth. "I was holding the coin. When I looked into the mirror, my image was not there. Nor was Merlin's. Instead it was yours! What were you doing, friend?"

"My thumb brushed over the surface of this old coin," said Jim, opening the fingers of his sweaty palm and showing the coin to Arthur.

Arthur said, "Why, yours looks like mine! This is a magic coin Merlin gave me when I was a child. When I wanted to talk with him, I couldn't always get to the big tree in the forest where he taught me my lessons as a child. If I needed to talk or if I had an emergency, I would brush my thumb from left to right over the word *Excalibur,* and then hold the coin in my hand. I would then find a shiny surface that reflects an image, like a mirror or a lake. As long as I held the coin, we could talk," responded Arthur.

"Excalibur!" said Jim to himself. Suddenly, Jim recalled the letters from the old coin. Jim no longer needed Vanna White to tell him what the missing letters were. *"That's* the word on the coin! *Excalibur!"* he blurted out loud, with joy, as if he had just won a round of *Wheel of Fortune!*

Arthur's surprise with Jim's excited outburst showed in the king's face. Jim tried to explain. "The letters on my coin are nearly worn away, Your Highness. I did not know the letters were from the word Excalibur until just now."

Suddenly the pilot's voice, screeching out of the airplane's loudspeaker, announced turbulence ahead. The pilot was going to fly at a higher altitude to escape the worst of the storm. All passengers were to return immediately to their seats and fasten their seat belts.

Arthur heard the announcement, but didn't understand its meaning. "Turbulence? Fly at a higher altitude? Seat belts? I have much to learn from you, my friend," exclaimed Arthur.

"And I the same, Your Majesty. Can we try this again at the same time tomorrow?"

"Agreed. I will be in the same place at the same time tomorrow, unless a battle ensues. I look forward to it eagerly, my friend."

The two men said good-bye. Jim returned to his seat, unaware of the smile on his face but very aware of the smile in his heart.

Excalibur

The glow of Jim's spirit matched the brilliant yellow, red, and orange autumn leaves just outside his living room window. It was early afternoon, and Jim had just arrived home from the airport. He was still savoring the rush from his meeting with King Arthur on the plane. At the same time, his body agonized from the assault of his long trip from London to Atlanta.

Like a small child, Jim could hardly wait until nightfall when he could speak with Arthur again. It seemed that Jim had a thousand questions to ask his royal mentor. And he wanted to ask every one of them *right now*! Waiting until then seemed like an eternity.

Jim took off his watch and placed it on the end table next to his sofa. His wallet came next, followed by the small cache of coins that had traveled with him from Europe. Among them was the magic coin that connected him to Arthur.

He picked up the magic coin and looked at it just as he had done several times throughout the day. He walked over to the large bay window on the west side of the room, and enjoyed how the sun's rays reflected off the coin.

As he stood looking out the window, Jim had a sudden flash of fear. "What if the coin doesn't work tonight? What if all this is just a dream?"

To soothe his anxious feelings, Jim decided to rehearse the process that was to connect him to his friend across the ages. Jim held the coin with the Excalibur side up, and then he brushed his thumb over it. The flash didn't startle him this time. Instead, it gave him comfort. He knew what to do to connect to his friend tonight.

"Great! It worked!" said Jim, not expecting to connect with Arthur yet. It wasn't time. As Jim turned away from the window to put the coin on the end table, though, there was Arthur looking at him through Jim's full-length wall mirror.

Instantly, both men broke out laughing. It was obvious to both that neither could wait until nightfall.

"I was eager to talk with you again, My Liege!" confessed Jim, still laughing. "I have too many questions I wanted to ask you. I was afraid the coin might not connect us. Talking with someone as important as you is like talking with Socrates or Plato. Tonight just seemed so far away."

Arthur was standing in his heavy suit of armor. His right hand pinched the magic coin. His left clutched the handle of the Sword Excalibur. Its blade plunged vertically from below Arthur's hand to cut its tip in the ground. "I was doing the same, my friend," Arthur said, his words sprinkled with laughter as well.

Arthur and Jim made some small talk for awhile. Each had such a high level of curiosity about the other that they stood opposite each other for nearly an hour. Their conversation stayed on comfortable topics. They talked about the differences in their clothing and their surroundings. *They even talked about sports!*

Then, prompted by a question from Arthur, Jim left the room briefly. He returned with a globe so he could show Arthur the world. Arthur was amazed at the big blue marble. He commented, "It is more beautiful than I could have ever imagined! I wish I could fly around it like an eagle, so I could explore all of it." That's when Jim told Arthur about airplanes, satellites, and spaceships.

Arthur's curiosity about the year 2000 seemed insatiable. He asked Jim what the box was on the other side of Jim's room. The box was a television set. Jim grabbed the remote control near him and then showed Arthur how it worked. Arthur was in awe of CNN, the Movie Channel, and *Jeopardy!*

"It is like having a thousand theater stages all at once! Oh, how much easier it would have been to lead if we had a device like a television in the year 597!"

Arthur unconsciously shifted his weight. At the same time, he moved the Sword Excalibur from his left hand to his right. The sword flashed as it caught a bright ray of light from a small bonfire that warmed Arthur in the chilly night air. Jim asked, "Sire! Is that the Sword Excalibur you have by you?"

"Yes *this* is Excalibur," said Arthur, quickly placing his weight on both feet. He hoisted the Sword Excalibur so it rested horizontally on top of both of his outstretched hands, allowing Jim a closer view.

Jim studied it, fascinated by Excalibur's elegant simplicity. The blade shone like a mirror. An intricate etched design decorated the entire length of the blade. The fire in Arthur's world sharpened the contrast between the shiny and dull surfaces of the blade. The contrast let Jim see the etched artwork clearly and appreciate its beauty. The detailed pattern reminded Jim of his sword from his days as a U.S. Marine, only Arthur's seemed even more glorious, and a lot heavier.

Excalibur's handle and hilt looked as if they were of a bright, shiny gold. They, too, were patterned. The handle had a deeply scored criss-cross pattern that gave Arthur a strong grip. Each criss-cross pattern was grooved into a diamond cut, making each point reflect the fire's light like a prism. From its golden handle, the hilt extended like a flagged horizontal top of a serif T. Excalibur had no jewels, nor did it need any.

"Sire, Excalibur was a very important part of the legend of your reign. Please tell me about Excalibur. Tell me of its magic power." Jim remembered some of the legend but wanted to know in Arthur's words what really happened.

Knowing Excalibur would take some explaining, Arthur suggested that both he and Jim sit down. They both did.

Arthur laid the sword on the ground in front of him, and then spoke. "In the time of my youth, all of England was in chaos. For nearly one hundred years, England was ruled by several kings. The first three of the kings had no greater interest than plundering the wealth of all who resided in this great land. Eventually, each was killed.

"A fourth king was a good king—at least for the people that lived in the king's castle. Outside of the castle walls, however, the fourth king was powerless to accomplish anything great to establish himself in history.

"The fourth king couldn't get the knights outside his walls to accept him as leader. Each knight's castle walls were like prisons of the mind. Thought was isolated and restricted by thick, impenetrable stone barriers. No matter how much he tried, the fourth king couldn't break through those barriers and get people in distant castles to join him.

"The fourth king was slain, too, by those outside his walls whose allegiance he did not win. Unfortunately, he was the last of the bloodline to the throne. Just before he took his last breath, though, the Lady of the Lake helped the good king cast Excalibur into a rock. Then she cast a spell on Excalibur. The spell froze the mighty sword in the rock until a great leader who could unite people across distance would magically have the power to free it.

"For about five years, England had no king. The throne sat empty, with no leader. Without leadership, England had only one ruler: chaos. Knights pitted against other knights in bloody battles for possessions and power. It did not matter that the people of England lived on one island countryside. Without leadership, every knight was out for himself."

The parallel between Arthur's description of England and Jim's project team was chillingly similar. All of the people on Jim's project team were supposedly united to achieve a business goal. But they really weren't united. People always made decisions based on local priorities. Jim even recalled doing that himself. Somehow local is a lot more tangible than global.

Arthur continued, "Since land, serfs, and other property were limited, a gain by one knight was always at the expense of another. The only world the knights cared about was the one they saw every day. The only trust they felt was to trust that someone would kill them when their guard was down."

Again, the parallel was almost too close for comfort. Just the other day, Jim got a call from Nicole, one of the Denver team players. Nicole was left out of the loop on a decision that had to be made. She was in a near panic at the hidden meaning behind that single act, saying, "Does this mean we should all be looking for jobs? How could you make a decision like this without consulting us first?"

Jim didn't intentionally leave Nicole out of the loop. The decision had to be made on the spot. Jim called her, but she was not at her desk. In his rush, he didn't leave a voice message. At that moment, Jim was forced to act, but he could hardly convince her otherwise. Later, she accused him of a power play, saying this was the third time it had happened. She had been increasingly hesitant to share information, not only with Jim but with anyone else on the team. There was a clear undertone of *screw them before they screw you* going on in the organization and in the team.

Arthur continued, "For decades, the kings that preceded me did little to change this bleak picture. By the time I was ten, war left a path of destruction so wide that the country exploited itself into darkness and economic collapse. Such was the England of my youth."

Jim was saddened by the gloomy picture Arthur had just painted, not just because of Arthur, but because of himself. Jim's company had downsized three times in the last two years. Profits were down. Rumors were flying that another cut was imminent. If Jim's team didn't do a better job of leveraging resources across distance in this project, the decline cycle would continue.

"Those sound like very dismal years, Sire," commented Jim.

Arthur responded. "Yes, they were. All of England waited for the moment in the sun when that great leader would arrive who could unite us and take us out of this desolation. In those same years, I did not know my destiny as a child. I did not know that Merlin was preparing me to be king.

"Later, when I was a squire, I had to fetch a sword for one of the knights who was about to duel. When I could not find the knight's sword, I tried to find another one. I saw a sword sticking out of a group of rocks, but did not know it was Excalibur. I was as surprised as anyone else when the sword slipped easily out of the hard stone that gripped it for so many years."

"Well, Your Majesty, did the sword magically give you the power you needed to lead?" questioned Jim.

"Excalibur did give me the *right* to lead. At that moment I, Arthur, a squire moments earlier, suddenly was King of England! There certainly was power in my position. As I stood there with the sword in my hand, the knights around me began to bow. I didn't want knights bowing to me. I didn't want followers who may do what I say and then kill me when I turn my back. *Position power means nothing if a leader fails to get everyone to join in.*

"Excalibur gave me another kind of power—lethal power. Excalibur was a weapon and could be used as such. If knights didn't do what I told them, I could kill them with it. I could threaten them and stick the blade in their throats. But I didn't want to use that kind of power either. Our people had suffered too long under the power of the sword. For a century that kind of power got us nowhere.

"So, to answer your question, Jim, at first I didn't know how the power of the sword would help me. This sword was to make me a great king, yet I had no idea how to get the process started.

"Later that night, I sneaked away from the camp and rode as fast as I could to the tree in the woods where Merlin taught me my most important lessons. I asked him how Excalibur was supposed to help me lead. What do I need to concentrate on to get people all over the country to become one? What do I need to remember that would make me successful in leading across distance?"

"What did he say?" said Jim, wanting to know the answer.

"In his deep, echoing voice, Merlin ordered me, 'First, Arthur, identify your enemies.' I thought he wanted me to give him the names of knights that were my foes.

"After some thought, I finally said to Merlin, 'I hardly *know* any of the knights. How can I identify them as my enemies?' I asked.

"Merlin seemed pleased with my response, at least at first. But then he sharply clarified himself, 'I did not want you to identify the *knights* you could not trust, Arthur. I want you to identify your *enemies*. Think, Arthur! *Think!*'

"My mind was racing as fast as it could. Merlin put such pressure on me at times to think differently about certain topics. I wanted to come up with the right answer, but all I was coming up with was a big blank.

"Merlin could see the answer wasn't imminent. So, he turned me into a hen. He often turned me into animals or plants to help me learn the lessons of life that were most important. So, in a flash, I was sitting on a straw nest on the top of an old tree stump. I was somewhere in the middle of a meadow of yellow wildflowers.

"The nest was warm, but uncomfortable. So I stood up to see what made the surface so lumpy. To my shock, there underneath me were three eggs! Merlin, still watching me, said, 'Each of these eggs bears the life of your dream of Camelot, Arthur. Just as a fox would rip the life from the eggs, you have three enemies that will rip the life from your dream. The enemies are *not* people, Arthur. They are something else. *What are your enemies*, Arthur?'

"I gently sat down on the eggs and thought for awhile. The image of the three eggs was swimming in my mind's eye. If the enemy wasn't people, the enemy had to be at a different level. So, within my mind, I stepped back to take a broader view.

"Finally the answers came. 'Merlin, I have it! I know the enemies to my leadership. First is *geography*. Geography makes the knights see themselves as separate from one another. Second is *isolation*. Isolation keeps them from knowing one another. The knights had no means of developing relationships with one another and benefiting from those relationships. Third is *history*. History makes them believe that the way distant knights have acted will be the way they will act forever.'

"Merlin lavished his praises on me. 'Excellent, Arthur! Correct! Your enemies, as remote leader, are geography, isolation, and history. *Whether you ignore them or accept them, any one or all of these enemies will smash the life out of the dream of Camelot. As king, you must always be on the offensive to defeat these enemies.'*

"Merlin then said to me, 'Just as the mother hen protects and nourishes her young, what do you need to do, as leader, to protect and nourish the dream of Camelot? What must happen for Camelot to smash the life out of the enemies of your leadership?'

"Again, my mind was whirling to find the answer. Now that the problem was identified, the solution came easier. In only a moment, I responded to Merlin, '*Geography* is a barrier, my teacher, but only a physical one. To counteract that barrier, I must create a very clear and compelling bond that unites knights from shore to shore. They must not see themselves as separate. Instead, they must see themselves as united together for some greater purpose. I must find a way to develop and nurture a sense of unity that is alive whether the people are with me or in their own castles.'

"Magically, Merlin changed one of the eggs to gold. On it he wrote *trusting unity*.

"Then I said, '*Isolation* is a barrier that keeps the knights from developing friendships and trust. Knights need friendships and trust to bond them when they are together, yet still be alive when they are apart. To counteract the barrier of isolation, I must make sure they have ways to learn about each other and get to know each other. Trusting relationships will let them be more open with one another and listen more effectively to each other. I must find ways to build and nourish trusting relationships among the knights and with me.'

"Merlin changed the second of the three eggs to gold. On it he wrote *trusting relationships*.

"Then I described the solution to the last problem. '*History* is both a teacher and a barrier. History brings rich lessons for all of us, and we need to always be open to its lessons. History is a tremendous barrier, though, when historical patterns must change. Changing history can be as frightening as the bloody massacre of battle.

"'To counteract that barrier, I must give the knights a new history—a future they can hold on to. That future must help them look beyond the narrow confines of each knight's individual castle to look at something greater. To earn their commitment, they must have a part in creating what that future will look like. For Camelot to work, everyone must have an unquestioning belief and commitment to making it happen. I have to find ways to keep high the trust in that future when knights are in their castles or in Camelot with me.'

"Merlin changed the third egg to gold. On it he wrote, *trusting shared future.*

"Merlin then changed me back into myself, but he left the three golden eggs in front of me. Excalibur was in my hands, but I still knew I did not know how to tap into the magic of the sword to lead from a distance. I knew my enemies. I knew what I needed to protect. As I stared at Excalibur, I still had more questions. Merlin had not yet let me discover how the sword would help me magically lead.

"Merlin must have read my mind, for he then said, 'Arthur, Excalibur is not magic. It has no magic power, nor do you. So don't try to wave Excalibur in the air and expect people magically to go along with you. Even *I* do not have that kind of magic!

"'There is a powerful magic available to you, though, *if* you pay attention to the message Excalibur will give you daily, Arthur. *The magic is not in the sword. It is what you create with people.* The sword is your reminder of your most important task as remote leader. If you discover the message of the sword, you will be able to create the magic you seek. So, look at the sword. Study it well, and you will have your answer!' "

At that point, Arthur stood up and held the sword vertically in front of Jim. The point of the sword dug into the ground, and the top was held in a light grip between Arthur's index finger and thumb. Then Arthur said to Jim, "What letter do you see in the sword?"

Seeing the blade and handle form a straight vertical line, and the hilt form a narrow horizontal one, Jim replied, "T. I see the letter T. But what does that mean, Your Majesty? How did Excalibur give you the power and control to make Camelot happen?"

Arthur responded, "It took me a while, but I finally figured out what T stood for. T was for trust. My chief role as remote leader was to build trust. I had to build trust in me as the remote leader. I had to build trust in Camelot. And most of all I had to build trust among the knights. *Knights who trust one another and like one another don't kill one another!*"

Jim was silent for a moment, madly trying to process what Arthur just said. Jim always viewed leadership as power and control which was used to get the task done. Building trust was on the list of important things for the leader to do, but it wasn't anywhere near the top.

Jim felt compelled to say to Arthur, "Your story is making me question some of my basic thoughts about leadership, Your Majesty. When you first showed me Excalibur, the first words that came to my mind were power and control. A leader must have power and control over people because the leader holds responsibility for the result. Your story doesn't even mention power and control. It only mentions trust. I don't understand why trust is so important when people are distant."

Arthur smiled and said, "I said the same thing to Merlin, Jim. If I were King, the only way I saw I could build Camelot was through power and control over people.

"So Merlin created two knights for my lesson, Sir

Bainbridge and Sir Kensington. He also made a duplicate set of eggs that looked and felt like gold, but wasn't. I met Sir Bainbridge at his castle and told him the three eggs I was about to give him to transport were the cornerstone of Camelot. I then gave him a command by the king's royal decree and the power of the Sword Excalibur. The royal charge was to guard the safekeeping of the eggs and deliver them to me at Camelot three days later. Separately, I did the same with Sir Kensington. Each of the knights then went out of my view. Sir Bainbridge had the imitation gold eggs, and Sir Kensington the real ones.

"There is no higher exercise of power and control I could humanly extend than to make a royal decree by the power of the Sword Excalibur. I am king. *My reign is supreme in all the land. When the knights are out of my view, though, my command has no power over them.* Neither I nor the Sword Excalibur can shadow the knight to make sure he does as he is bidden."

Jim asked, "Then, Your Majesty, was there any way to guarantee the eggs would arrive safely?"

"Yes, Jim, there is a way—through *trust*. If I wanted my royal decree carried out while any knight was out of my view, the knight and I first had to establish a mutual level of trust. The knight had to trust me, and I him. The knight had to trust in the dream of Camelot. And the knight had to trust that his royal charge to protect the eggs was important.

"Sir Bainbridge and I did not take the time to build trust before he left my view. We had no bond. Although he never spoke it to my face, he didn't trust I would be king for more than a year. He didn't believe Camelot would ever happen. He thought the royal order of knights was a farce. On the first day he was out of my view, Sir Bainbridge laughed as he sold the golden eggs for a hefty profit. Without trust, my command to him was powerless across distance.

"On the other hand, Sir Kensington not only kept all three eggs safe, but he did a great deal more. He built a beautiful case to safely house the golden eggs while in transit. He engaged his most trusted servants to protect him. During the entire three-day journey, he never left the eggs out of his view.

"With Sir Kensington, I took the time to build and assure trust before he left my presence. We found common interests that linked us as humans. I was careful that my every word and every action showed my true commitment as king to Camelot. Before Sir Kensington left, he trusted me, the dream of Camelot, and the important new role of knights. *Once he was out of my sight, the only power and control I had as king was what the knight exercised over himself. Only with a bond of trust could I be assured of the result I wanted.*"

Jim looked at the Sword Excalibur, let his eyes be reminded of the T shape, and said, "So, Your Majesty, trust enabled you to get the result you wanted, and a whole lot more. Because of trust, Sir Kensington not only delivered the eggs. He took the initiative to do much more than you asked. Trust let him embrace his important task and take personal responsibility for its success. He exercised power and control over himself."

Arthur then interjected, "That's right, Jim! Trust is at

the core of leading any group that spans distance. It is important to know, though, that when knights come from great distances, they don't have the opportunity to develop trust to the same level as if they all frequented the same castle each day.

"With the Knights of the Round Table, I always saw trust as fragile as an egg shell dropped on a rock. *To be a successful king, every word, every action, every initiative I spoke had to build trust.* There must never be a doubt about trust, especially where you are concerned, as leader."

Jim reflected on the incident with Nicole again. Her words reflected a number of trust issues that Jim blew off earlier but now knew were serious, indeed. Jim knew he needed to learn more specifics from Arthur about how to build trust.

Jim said, "Building trust across distance is easier said than done, Sire. There are so many opportunities for trust issues to surface when people are distant. When people work in one location, they can see what is going on. When people work across distance, they don't. Lacking all the needed information, they'll fill in the blanks! And that's when trouble begins, because they don't always fill in the blanks correctly. People make negative assumptions about each other that have no basis in fact." As he spoke, Jim remembered Nicole's accusation that Jim had never called her, along with all of the negative assumptions that went with her lack of trust.

Arthur said, "Building trust across distance *is* difficult, but achievable, Jim. Today, we've just covered some of the highlights. We'll need a lot more time to talk about them in more detail. As you'll see, though, *every factor critical to your success across distance comes back to the fragile issue of trust.*"

Arthur was distracted for a moment in his world. Some knights were looking for him and were calling his name. Arthur said to Jim, "Some of my knights are summoning me. Before I leave, Jim, I want to tell you one more story about Merlin. Remember, I rode deep into the woods to talk with him to tap into the magic of Excalibur to help me lead across distance.

"With all of his great wisdom, Merlin made this important point to me. He said, 'Leadership is not something you do *to* someone, Arthur. It is something you do *for* them. If you try to exercise power and control over people, you are doing something *to* them. You are inflicting your will on them and you are making them rely on you. When people are distant, this approach is deadly.

"'On the other hand, if you build trust, you are doing something *for* them. You are helping them to rely on their own unique talents, abilities, and perspectives. You are trusting them to tap into the power and control within themselves. If they trust you, the dream of Camelot, and the power of their union with one another as people, you'll be richly rewarded. Just remember Sir Kensington.'

" The sword, Jim, has always been my constant reminder of my most important task as leader: build trust. Trust is what let the Knights of the Round Table and I build Camelot. In retrospect, I also know a breach of trust is what made it fall."

Jim wanted to make sure he clearly heard his royal mentor's key points. He said, "If I relate what you have said to my project, Your Majesty, I have to be very sensitive to the fragile levels of trust that are in place when people work across distance. The slightest word or act, that wouldn't breach trust if people knew each other well, can be very damaging when people lack solid relationships.

"Therefore, my chief role as project leader is to build trust in me, in the project, and in a unified team, despite distance. I have to make sure that my every word, every act, and every gesture builds trust in me as the leader. I have to build trust that by working together, my knights and I can build a future we all want. And I have to create ways for my knights to develop trust with each other."

Arthur responded, "Exactly! Only when trust flourishes, do people do magically wonderful things together, like create Camelot!"

Jim looked forward to learning more from Arthur. He wanted to know more precisely how Arthur built high levels of trust across distance with his Knights of the Round Table.

Jim and Arthur set a time to meet the following morning, thanked each other for a wonderful session, and then said farewell.

Jim's view of leadership made a substantial shift after this session. No longer could he see leadership as power and control over people. Now leadership meant something more important, exciting, and challenging to him! He felt more comfortable understanding how to get power and determine his desired result through building trust.

In his mind's eye, Jim saw Excalibur. He read the T of its shape. And he knew the key factor he had to concentrate on to be successful as remote leader.

The Round Table

Over the next day, Jim began to pay close attention to his communication. For the first time in his life, Jim realized that every time people communicate, trust is built or lost. His conversations with others were no longer just exchanges of information and data. Now they were also barometers of trust and anchors that bind people together to get results.

With E-mail, voice mail, and the void of distance, Jim also realized every time people didn't communicate effectively or didn't communicate at all, trust is impacted. Jim knew he had a lot more to learn about the fine points of how trust is built and destroyed.

After skipping a day, Jim and Arthur decided to meet the following morning. Since Arthur didn't have a watch, the two men gauged the beginning of their meeting by the sunrise. To the best that they could coordinate a time, Jim figured the meeting would begin about 7:00 A.M. Atlanta time.

"Perfect!" said Jim to himself. He had a surprise in mind for his royal mentor. At their previous meeting, Arthur had the curiosity of a child while listening to Jim's stories of a modern day world. Like a sponge, he hung on Jim's every word, trying to understand the new concept he learned about: the high-tech world of the year 2000.

There was only so much technology Jim could show Arthur from his home. So, Jim's next treat to his royal mentor was to show him a different part of life in the year 2000. Jim planned to take Arthur on his morning commute to the office. Jim wanted Arthur to feel the exhilaration of traveling down I-75 at highway speed. He wanted Arthur to enjoy the beauty of the highway as it wove up and down, left and right, across Georgia's beautiful wooded countryside. Jim thought to himself, "I'll link with Arthur at 65 miles per hour. That should get a reaction!"

At 7 A.M., the light turned green for Jim to enter the on-ramp to I-75. As soon as Jim's car was up to highway speed, Jim took out the magic coin and brushed his thumb over the word Excalibur. As expected, Arthur popped into sight in Jim's rearview mirror. He looked at Jim, smiling, ready to greet his friend from the future. Before Arthur could say hello, though, Arthur's eyes were drawn like magnets to the scene behind Jim.

The look that then appeared on Arthur's face was priceless! Arthur knew his mouth was hanging open in wonder, and he didn't care! The only part of the scene that Arthur recognized were the trees. Those he saw through the side windows were whizzing by at such speed, all Arthur could see was a blur of green.

The real surprise for Arthur was another big chunk of Jim's world that Arthur's royal eyes had never seen. Arthur's attention was lured like a fish toward an array of strange, colorful objects that dotted his view. Dozens of colorful vehicles passed Jim's with the swiftness of eagles. Some of the vehicles were round, some were square. Some were big and some were small. And some were even wedge-shaped like cheese.

The vehicles were painted in colors as bright as the rainbows that hung over Camelot. They all traveled faster than foxes in the woods. Arthur surprised himself by his reflexed *oh's* and *ah's* as the strange vehicles passed Jim in a flash, and as Jim passed others. How exciting and fast-moving this new world was!

As Jim rounded a curve on the highway, traffic suddenly came to a halt. Jim quickly stepped on the brake, as did all of the cars beside and behind him. The sound of squealing brakes filled the air.

Suddenly, cars several lengths behind Jim quickly decelerated to a stop. In fractions of a second cars quickly closed in. The cars appeared to Arthur as if they were about to crash into Jim's. The strangeness of the sound, the rapid stop, and the sudden closeness of the cars behind Jim made Arthur curl his arms to protect his face. Arthur was reflexively waiting for a crash that never came.

Once silence returned to the road, silence also filled

the inside of the car. And then he and Jim both began to laugh. Laughter instantly diffused the tension of the near-collision stop.

Arthur finally spoke. "Where are you? What is this place, Jim? What are these strange things I see that move so fast but now are stopped?"

Jim began this journey wanting to introduce Arthur to more of his high-tech world. It was clear now that Arthur would get the *real* indoctrination to the year 2000: gridlock and traffic jams!

Jim then responded to Arthur's question. "Welcome to a common failing of the year 2000, Your Majesty. We are in my car. My car is stuck in a traffic jam on I-75. And so are several hundred or so cars in back and in front of me," said Jim, hoping no one could see him talking to his rearview mirror. Jim quickly looked at the cars in the lanes to his left and right. The drivers seemed preoccupied with other distractions and weren't looking at Jim.

"In a car? What is a car?" asked Arthur.

"A car is a form of transportation. You might say it is a modern day version of a horse and chariot, all in one," said Jim.

"Excuse me, but I don't see any horses! What happened to horses in the year 2000?"

"Well, they're under the hood, Your Majesty . . . uh, kind of. The horses you are familiar with are still around, but there is a new kind of horse that was invented about a hundred years ago—*horsepower*. My car has the power of 240 horses under the hood.

"In a traffic jam like this, horsepower isn't used well.

But on a road without traffic, *wow*, Arthur! Well, you saw how this beauty goes! It shoots like an arrow down the highway. If there were no other cars on the road and if we were on a road like this in England, I could travel from the farthest point north to the farthest point south in only a few hours!"

Most of the words and description Jim gave went right over Arthur's head. Arthur didn't understand how horsepower was *invented* when horses were *born*. He didn't understand the words *traffic* or *highways* very clearly. And he didn't like the brownish cloud that hovered over the trees. Rather than having Jim explain it now, though, Arthur stayed with Jim's last sentence about travel time.

"A few hours! Why, that journey would take someone in my time several days. It takes one day to see Sir Dinadan or five to see Sir Sagramore. A trip to see Sir Lionel takes about two weeks. Why, even Lancelot's trip from France took nearly a month! Distance is an enormous barrier in my time."

Jim responded, "For me to travel from England to Atlanta, it only took eight hours of flight, Your Majesty. Even with cars, planes, and a lot of other technologies I use every day, though, distance is *still* a barrier in the year 2000," lamented Jim.

"Why, a couple of days ago, when you identified the three enemies of geography, isolation, and history, I thought you were describing my project team. Those same enemies haunt my project team, even today! It is tough to get people that are distant to create trusting relationships. It's tough to get them to see beyond their own castles.

"Your Majesty, the people on my project aren't acting or working as a unit, like your Knights of the Round Table did. Distance isolates the people on my project from each other and from me.

"In fact, isolation is such a common problem that we have given it a name—*remotitis*! People on the project see themselves as isolated pieces, not a cohesive whole.

"If I'm lucky, the people on my project will cooperate with each other. Cooperation, though, isn't enough. For my project to be successful, the team must collaborate and share resources across distance. Right now, they're not leveraging anything.

"I just don't know how you confronted the barriers to build the Knights of the Round Table into a cohesive unit. I'm beginning to believe that the only way I can create an energized, cohesive team is to move them to one location," confessed Jim. Jim knew that moving everyone to one location was not an option, but he wished it were.

Arthur responded, "I know the isolation of which you speak, my friend. For hundreds of years, isolation kept the knights all over England locked in separate worlds. Isolation kept them caught up in their local concerns, with no regard for the whole of England. Isolation justified their view of *outsiders* as enemies from other castles that could not be trusted. I knew I had to change that," said Arthur.

Jim, eager to hear how Arthur broke through the barrier of distance, asked, "What was the situation like when you first tried to unite the knights? How did you get them to see themselves as one group? How did you get them to

— 48 —

trust one another when they didn't see each other often and when they had such a divisive history?" asked Jim.

Arthur said, "To answer your questions, Jim, I must begin at an earlier experience in my life. Let me take you back to my childhood to another of my lessons from Merlin.

"From the time I was a small child, I remember stories of great knights who distinguished themselves in the glory of battle. Although the people of England didn't travel much from castle to castle, legends of knights in battle did. Tales of the knights' triumphs and the defeats rang out throughout the countryside. As the stories echoed throughout the land, the glory of battle became even more glorified.

"One day, I asked Merlin to show me the *glory* of battle. I was 12, and I could not wait any longer to get a firsthand view of what *glory* was all about. Now that I was considered a young man, Merlin obliged. He wove his magic to make both of us and our horses invisible. Then we rode into the countryside to find a battle in progress.

"As the horses rounded the top of a rolling hillside, we could see in the distance that a battle was about to begin. Two knights, mounted on their horses, faced each other. Each of the knights was flanked by about ten squires who had lesser weapons but were also prepared to go to battle.

"The knights on each side of the battle did not know each other. Other than the threatening words they spoke before the battle, the knights had never talked with each other. Dressed in full battle armor, the knights could not see each other's faces."

Arthur's words triggered a picture of the faceless person Jim spoke with on the telephone yesterday. It was a person Jim didn't know who seemed to push Jim for a decision. Jim remembered how easy it was to be rude to someone who was a non-person, just a voice on the phone. He didn't need a reason to fight a non-person just as the knights in Arthur's time didn't need much of a reason to fight each other.

In Jim's role as leader, he had to do battle with many people he never met personally. It was so easy to be curt or even rude to those he had never met before and might never meet again. It was so normal to distrust a voice on the phone that wasn't from a familiar face. Jim wondered how many others shared those same perceptions.

Arthur continued, "Suddenly, one of the knights made the first move. In a flash, both became fully engaged in a ferocious, brutal battle. Swords and other battle weapons were whipping, slashing, and piercing to the hilt. The squires joined in.

"Painful screams and groans filled the air as one by one the opponents killed their nameless foes. In minutes, the beautiful emerald grass turned a bitter color of red that I would never be able to erase from my memory, no matter how hard I tried. For a century, battle was a way of life. Hundreds of knights and swordsmen killed and maimed each other in the name of *glory*."

For a flash, Jim saw the glory of globalization. Then he saw the nameless victims of the battle for the bottom line. Suddenly the faces of these modern-day knights were clearly visible to Jim. Their faces showed fear of being slashed in the next downsize or eliminated if they shared information. There was no glory in competition for survival between sites. There was only further destruction of jobs and opportunities.

Arthur continued, "When we came across the carnage of battle, I knew that such destruction was nothing to be revered. Glory is not a word I could associate with battle; *gory* was. It made my heart ache to see such devastation.

"At that moment I turned to my mentor, Merlin. I asked him what was the key to peace and prosperity among the knights. What could a king do to change this divisive pattern and get them to unite as one?

"Merlin rarely answered my questions directly. He didn't want to tell me the answer. Instead, he said I would learn the answer better if I discovered it myself. To find the key to peace, he turned me into an eagle. He told me to fly wherever I wanted until I could see the answer.

"At the beginning of my flight, I was queasy about soaring so high in the air. But once I got the hang of it, flying was exhilarating, just like the car ride was this morning—at least when we were moving! Soaring above the earth gave me a different perspective that opened my eyes and my mind.

"My wings let me soar high above England's beautiful meadows and forests. My broad wings let me glide past many fortressed castles. Finally, I located the castle of one of the knights that had just been killed in *glorious* battle. I flew among the rafters of his castle. I admired the beautiful community the knight had built at home. The knight had a loving wife and six children who wept at the news of his death. So did all of the other people who were in the good knight's service.

"I flew to the opposing knight's castle. To my surprise, the opposing knight also had created a beautiful yet very different community at home. The people in the opposing knight's castle also wept at news of his loss.

"What a waste battle was! These two knights who died in battle never talked with one another. They did not know how much they had in common. They did not know how much they could learn from each other, nor how they could prosper together!

"As long as the knights didn't know each other, it was easy for them to be enemies. It was easy for them to stay in their separate worlds. It was easy for them to distrust each other. Their divisive past kept them from seeing any benefit they could gain from each other. *Distance was the perfect curtain to keep them apart and maintain their distrust of each other.*

"So distraught by what I saw, I flew elsewhere over the countryside. The same patterns repeated themselves. As I swooped down into each of the castles, I listened to the conversations of the people. It was clear that the walls limited the people's perspective, just as the walls of my castle limited mine. All of the knights resided on the same island countryside, but nobody cared and *nobody benefitted from it.*"

"So, what did you learn from your flight as an eagle, My Liege?" questioned Jim.

"I learned that castle walls are artificial boundaries. Soaring above the countryside, I could see that in life there are no boundaries other than those we set in our minds. If I wanted to unite the knights across distance, I had to change the knights' thinking and also my own.

"First I had to believe myself that geography was not a barrier. Then I had to help the knights see there were no boundaries either. I had to help them define a new linkage that bridged the distance among all of them. *That new linkage had to offer a lot more to each knight than what they had without it.*"

Despite technology, Jim always felt geography *was* a barrier. In the back of his mind, Jim never really thought of his project team as a *team*. To him, and many other leaders in the company, teamwork was a one-roof, one-company phenomenon. Jim felt more like a leader of several separate teams, rather than one project team where people spanned the world. In general, the people on the team didn't think high performance could be achieved across distance either.

Jim tried to compensate for distance by developing a thorough project plan. In fact, the plan was so complete and detailed, he felt it almost guaranteed an excellent result, worldwide. The problem was the plan wasn't working. People on the team were drawn more to local projects and local events than they were to Jim's worldwide project.

In the ideal, Jim felt Arthur's words made perfect sense. Walls of castles are artificial boundaries. With globalization and technology, so are walls of the business unit, the corporate buildings, and even meeting rooms themselves.

Jim knew the *real* world, though, is far from the *ideal* that Arthur described. People in the year 2000 have a whole array of tools to communicate quickly and easily across distance. *The tools were important, but they clearly weren't enough to create a high performance partnership with people across distance.* Jim needed to find something more to truly get people on his worldwide project team to unite.

Jim asked Arthur, "How *did* you get the knights from their distant locations to feel linked and united as a group, Your Majesty?"

Arthur thought for a moment. "Knights are naturally more drawn to the needs and interests of their local castles than they are to a group that meets only once in a while. I had to become very creative in finding clear and concrete ways the knights could identify with one another at a different level. Clear and concrete symbols had to replace the face to face interaction the knights missed with one another.

"I can think of two key strategies that were important to bond the knights in purpose and to each other, across distance. First was to create strong, visible symbols of the knights' linkage across distance. The first and most important symbol was to give the leadership group a name, Knights of the Round Table."

Jim interjected, "Knights of the Round Table is such a memorable and terrific name, Your Majesty. How did you think of it?"

Arthur said, "Actually, the name Knights of the Round Table arose from a battle I had with Sir Sagramore shortly after I became king.

"After Excalibur gave me the right to lead, some knights gave me their allegiance instantly. Winning allegiance from many other knights, though, took a lot more effort. I had no reputation in the land, as some of the other knights had. So I had to win the allegiance of each of the disbelieving knights, one by one, in battle.

"The first knight who challenged me was Sir Sagramore. I asked him to join me in a new order of knights. In my lofty language, I told him he could be a part of creating a new England that was exciting and different and wonderful. His response was to knock down my words with his cutting tongue, and then knock down my body with his sword!

"Knowing my life was in danger, I quickly sprang back to my feet. Then, for a time that seemed like an eternity, Sagramore and I both fought valiantly with swords and battle axes. Our skills were well-matched as each had the advantage over the other several times during the battle.

"In a last-ditch effort to end the endless battle, I mustered every bit of energy left in my body and struck the final blow. My sword knocked Sagramore briskly and firmly to the ground. We had fought so long, though, I fell to the ground almost immediately after him.

"For several minutes, both of us could do little more than try to find enough air to breathe into our energy-spent bodies. We were too exhausted to speak or move.

"Finally, after I caught enough breath, I said to him, 'You have great strength, Sir Sagramore. I have never met a challenger with such tenacity and skill. You can put your strengths to better use than in a battle like this. I want you to be a part of a new order of knights that I am leading as England's king. We will do battle in a new way that doesn't kill off our strengths.'

"Sagramore looked sharply at me. His eyes showed anger and hope at the same time. He said, 'You use so many vague words! A *new* order of knights! I've heard those meaningless words before! You have beaten me here in battle today, *Sire*. As such, I am required to do as you bid. But I cannot pledge you my unfaltering allegiance to something so vague and meaningless! I want to know in specific terms what you want me to join, what you plan to do with it, and how it benefits *me*!'

"Sagramore was right. I was too vague. He was looking for something more concrete and specific than I had yet described. The group needed a name.

"As my mind scrambled to find a name, my mind's eye took me to the tree in the forest where Merlin taught me my lessons of life. Some of the lessons were taught at a small round table Merlin built for my learning. Merlin would bring famous thinkers like Plato and Aristotle to the table to talk with me and open my mind.

"The table was round for another reason. Merlin told me the table was to remind me to think and communicate in circular ways. 'What goes around, comes around,' he always used to say."

Jim thought to himself, "Amazing! My mom, dad,

and teachers are still saying those words 1400 years later! In fact, I've said it to my children, too!"

Arthur continued, "With that circular table in mind, I blurted out, 'Sir Sagramore, I want you to become a Knight of the *Round* Table.'

"With those words, Sagramore sat up and raised his eyebrows. His face told me I got his attention. The words made my ambiguous group become more concrete and specific. The name made something intangible now more tangible."

Jim said, "So, giving a group that spans distance a name that defines what they are or what they are doing is critical."

Arthur responded, "Yes, Jim, but there's more. The name had to carry a lot of meaning to the knight. Expectations about the group had to be high enough to capture the interest and commitment of each of the knights.

"Sagramore and I talked at length about the Round Table. I let him know it was an honor to accept the challenge of the noble charter to create Camelot together. I was looking for people who were as committed as I to make Camelot happen. Building Camelot was not just for me and my glory. It was for each knight, the people of his castle, and the people over all of England, as well."

Jim summarized, "So the Round Table was more than a name. *You attached a great deal of prestige and value to the knights' important role in being a part of something special.*"

When Arthur answered in the affirmative, Jim realized he had never taken the time with his team to have them discuss the importance of this project or their role in it, in their own terms. In fact, he never stated his own commitment, nor did he tell the team about commitment higher in the organization for the project. He made a mental note to do that and then gave Arthur a nonverbal signal to continue his story.

Arthur said, "Then Sagramore asked, *'How will I benefit from being a Knight of the Round Table?'* His question turned out to be one of the most important factors that created the commitment across distance I was looking for.

"If I wanted a knight's committed service—whether near or far from me—he individually had to benefit. If I wanted him to work with *all* of his heart and *all* of his strength during *all* of the time he would serve at a distance, he had to feel deep personal commitment to it. Only *he* could define those factors that would win him to the Round Table. So I asked him, 'What benefit do you seek, Sir Sagramore?'

"He responded, 'I want to take a leadership role in contributing something meaningful. I want you to give me the chance to do that. Even though my castle is in this remote place, *I want you to listen to my ideas and to use my knowledge.* I want my contribution to be *known* to people at my castle and to *benefit* the people of my castle. Most of all, I want your commitment that you will do everything you can as leader to make the Round Table succeed.'

"I quickly said, 'You have my pledge for all of these things, Sir Sagramore, *Knight of the Round Table.*' We took off our gloves and sealed our pledge to the partnership by shaking hands."

Jim's project plan covered the topic of gaining world-wide commitment. According to that plan, each person's commitment was to the team first, the organization second, and to the individual third. Now Jim knew the priority he wrote was backward. The most important commitment Jim needed was at the individual level first. The worldwide project would be successful only if personal commitment from each team member stayed high, despite their isolation across distance.

Jim had never asked each of the members on the project how he or she would benefit by being a part of it. Jim realized that he may have missed an opportunity to raise their commitment to the project, to the team, and to him as its leader. He decided to take the time to do that with each person on the team. Now, though, he wanted to ask Arthur about a more pressing question.

Jim asked, "Sir Sagramore said he wanted a *leadership* role at the Round Table, Sire. How can any group with a king have more than one leader?"

Arthur responded, "The challenge of creating Camelot was immense, Jim. I knew what I wanted for Camelot, but I did not know all of the answers. I could not see all of the details. I did not have all of the perspectives.

"Camelot's *real* glory came from the leadership of every one of the knights. *Their* ideas and *their* perspectives enriched Camelot and made it great. Remember, leadership is something a leader does *for* the knights. What the Round Table did *for* the knights was to give them many opportunities to learn, grow, and demonstrate their leadership. It gave them many chances to work together and build trust. *As leader, I could not afford to ignore any knight's ideas.*

"There is another key point, though, Jim, that is important. Knights were *not* expected to come to the table as followers of me. Followers had no place at the Round Table. We had too much to do. We had too much distance to cover. Besides that, distance didn't let me supervise knights split all over England.

"Camelot's success needed the leadership of each and every knight. I counted on each knight's ideas at the Round Table. I needed each knight's leadership to create Camelots in castles throughout all of England. Otherwise, Camelot never would have happened or been as glorious!"

Jim interjected, "In my time, we have a concept called empowerment, Your Majesty. With empowerment, the leader shares his or her power with others on the team.

"It sounds like you went beyond empowerment. You did share your power with your knights. But, more importantly, it sounds like *you built your leadership power base by accessing the power each knight already had as a leader of his own castle.*"

Arthur answered, "You are very perceptive, Jim. Camelot's success required leadership from shore to shore. No one leader is powerful enough or bright enough to do it alone. Even as king, I didn't have enough power to share to make Camelot happen. My role as leader was to capture the knights' power and talent by joining them together for a greater purpose.

"Make no mistake, Jim. *As king, I had the most power.*

I was in charge. However, I increased my power by tapping into the powerful leadership of each of the knights—every time I could. If you regard your knights as leaders, you'll treat them—and their ideas—differently than if you look at them as followers. And so will they."

Jim had always looked at the concept of team as a leader with followers. At the Round Table, Arthur had no followers. *Arthur positioned himself as a leader of leaders.* The Round Table was a leader*full* team aimed at channeling the energy of the knights to create Camelot together.

Jim interjected, "So the Round Table was a table of leaders not followers. What a wonderful idea, Your Majesty! Please tell me more about how you strengthened the bond of the knights to the Round Table?"

Arthur answered, "Because knights mostly lived in their own castles and traveled to Camelot rarely, we needed symbols to remind us of our linkage. At the first meeting, every knight received a ring that identified him as one of the Knights of the Round Table.

"The ring stood as a symbol of many discussions of their important leadership mission. The ring reminded the knight, whether in Camelot or in his castle, of his linkage to other knights. It also stood as a visible symbol to others throughout all of England that the knights were united in purpose."

Jim knew his team wouldn't wear rings, but he clearly understood Arthur's message. Symbols are important. *Since his project team didn't have a physical space they shared and worked at each day, they did need something tangible and symbolic to identify them as a unified group.*

"As we reached significant events in creating Camelot, the knights received other visible symbols to celebrate and recognize their accomplishments together as knights. As we completed key parts of Camelot, I called the knights to the Round Table. We congratulated each other on individual and group successes. And then every knight would get another symbol that celebrated their joint success.

"I remember one time I gave them a blanket to decorate their horse. The blanket had each knight's individual crest on one side, and the Round Table symbol on the other. Jim, the point to remember is that the knights didn't just get gifts from me. Instead, they received *symbols of their accomplishments as Knights of the Round Table.*"

Jim summarized what he heard. "So, the Knights of the Round Table began with a symbol that identified them as a group. As they worked together, you added many more symbols of their accomplishments *as a group.* You intentionally used symbols visible to the knights, whether in Camelot or in their castles. In addition, you also planned the symbols to also be visible to others throughout all of England."

Arthur shook his head in agreement, and said, "The more the knights created together as Knights of the Round Table, the more visible and united they became as a group. All of that was part of my plan to unite them."

Jim never believed in trinket management. He knew that giving his project team members a T-shirt doesn't make them a team. However, he liked the idea of giving his worldwide team a name or symbol identity. And he liked the idea of awarding additional team symbols with milestones. *Symbols somehow turned the team no one could see to one that was clear to identify in name and in accomplishments.*

Jim had built clear goals and milestones into his project plan. He made a mental note to do something about strengthening the symbolism on his team. He decided to add specific rewards and recognition into the project plan, so all team members worldwide could celebrate their success together.

Most of all, Jim could see he needed a world of leadership to bring his project to success. He liked the concept of being a leader of leaders, not followers.

The Joust

Still on the commute to work, Jim's car finally passed the accident that caused the traffic snarl. In seconds, Jim was back to highway speed.

Jim continued the conversation with Arthur, changing the topic slightly. "Your Majesty, all that you have shared with me about the Round Table makes sense. They are techniques I can, and will, use with my team.

"I still have a rather significant concern that I want to talk with you about. Once you got the knights to the Round Table, how did you get them to talk and not do battle with each other? It is one thing to create the Round Table. It's another to get people to communicate with each other at it. How did you get them to exchange words, not death blows?"

Arthur responded, "I had the same concern when I

planned the first meeting at the Round Table, Jim. If the knights were to unite as a single group, it was not enough for the knights to sit around a table. I wanted *real* openness. I wanted *real* listening. I wanted *real* energy. None of these would happen unless I created an environment at the Round Table that allowed openness to flourish.

"Getting the knights to communicate openly with one another was one of my most difficult tasks. Let me tell you the challenge I faced at the first meeting at the Round Table.

"Some 60 knights traveled from all over England to Camelot for the first meeting of the Round Table. Knights arrived in full battle armor, complete with swords. There was such excitement, yet such tension in the room as the five-day meeting began.

"Introductions were made by everyone seated around the table. When Sir Lionel stood to say his name, another knight three seats away, stood and said, 'How dare this outlaw sit at this distinguished table? Lionel is a thief and a murderer who plundered a peasant village for no just cause. He has nothing to say that I want to hear.'

"In a flash, Lionel drew his sword, challenging his accuser to battle. Lionel retorted, 'You are a liar, nameless knight! I challenge you to battle to prove your accusation! Or shall we do battle to let God decide who is right?'

"Jim, here we were only beginning the introductions to start the first meeting at the Round Table when the battle challenge was made.

"I instantly realized how difficult it was going to be to conduct this first meeting! The meeting had barely started, and the knights were ready to resort to old habits—deadly combat. These two knights were drawing limits to their communication and interaction by drawing swords. In this instant, I saw all of my effort and work collapsing in one gigantic battle.

"As my eyes scanned the knights seated around the table, I sensed underlying distrust throughout the room. I knew some of the distrust was based on real history. Some was based on rumor and legend. But most, in my view, was because the knights did not know each other yet.

"They were *uncomfortable* with each other. In contrast, they were very *comfortable* with their swords and battles. It's the only pattern they knew.

"The tension of my hand's grip on Excalibur told me this issue of trust was not to be ignored. So I bolted out of my chair. In a flash, I climbed onto the top of the Round Table. With Excalibur in hand, I stopped when I reached the center of the enormous table. I plunked the blade into the table top, and I walked around it as I spoke."

In his mind's eye, Jim pictured Arthur's imposing presence standing at the center of the Round Table. Jim pictured a huge table, crafted in a pie-slice design, with each slice of a different type of wood, finished to perfection.

"Shocked by my move, knights throughout the room became still. I said, '*You* are Knights of the Round Table. Every one of *you* has earned the right to sit around it because of your great deeds. Every one of *you* has pledged your commitment to me *and* to the task we join together to create.

" 'Most of you are new to each other today. Each knight in this room comes from a different part of England. Each shares a unique history. Each speaks with a different accent. Each has different strengths unknown to others in this room, including me. Each of us has fought different battles. Some of you have even fought each other.

" 'For all of these things that divide us, so many are rooted in our destructive past. So many are rooted in all that we do not yet know of each other.'

"Then I spoke to the knights about my flight as a bird. I recounted my search with Merlin for *glory*. Then I said to the knights, 'Real glory is in what all of you, as Knights of the Round Table, can build together. It is no longer found in those things that kept you apart.

" 'In order to build a glorious future for England, we must build trust with one another. We must get to know each other as humans, not strangers. We must move our need to do battle away from the Round Table.

" 'Our time together will always be limited. So, all of us are challenged to build trust and rapport quickly. We'll also be challenged to trust one another as honorable knights who were brought to this table by me, your king.

" 'If we are to be successful, it is critical to remember the words I say to you now. *Trust until you have a clear and specific reason to distrust. Then talk about it without accusing each other. Just state what you observed, and let the other knight fill in the details you will not have.' "

Jim thought of how many times he distrusted strangers. Arthur was asking for a big leap of faith—to trust, rather than distrust—those who are not known well to each other. Jim could see, though, how operating with an assumption of trust, rather than distrust, would change the spontaneous reaction of everyone on the team.

Jim's mind tallied the huge amount of unclear and incomplete information across distance. How different it would be to hear "When I didn't hear from you at 3:00, I knew something important must have happened," rather than "Why did you deliberately leave me out of the loop." Jim made a mental note to bring the idea of a trust assumption to his team.

Arthur continued, "Then I reminded the knights of my commitment of openness to them. Still standing in the middle of the table, I said, 'As your king, I do not care if you reside in any of the castles that border mine, or if you travel from castles located in the farthest shores of England. I do not care if you come from the largest castle or the smallest. You are all here because you have something important you can contribute to making Camelot happen. All of us have much to learn from each other.

" 'This table is round for a reason. It is symbolic of the ring that binds us. Equally as important, it is symbolic of the circle of communication. For all of us, if we want respect, first we must give respect. If we want trust, first we must give trust. If we want to be heard, first we must listen. If we want to speak, first we must let others speak.

" 'At the Round Table, no knight has a greater voice than any other knight. You have my pledge as King that while we sit at the Round Table, your ideas will always be heard and valued. I expect the same from each one of you.'

"Complete silence filled the room. I knew I had struck an important chord by addressing the issue of trust right away. One by one I looked at the eyes of every knight who circled the table. Every one was looking at me, awaiting my next words.

"After the long silence, I finally said, 'We sit at the Round Table to exchange ideas, not swords. We are here *not* as enemies. Instead, we are here as great knights who will become trusted friends.'

"The knights clapped! Then they stood and clapped some more! When silence again came back to the room, I instituted a ceremony that we used to begin all of our meetings at the Round Table. The purpose of the ceremony was to remind everyone that the Round Table symbolized a place where ideas and ideals were valued.

"On the command, each of the knights reached for his sword. In unison, each drew his sword and presented it symbolically to the group. Reciting after me, the knights reminded themselves they were laying down their swords in exchange for the right to be heard.

"The swords were then placed on the table in front of each of the knights. The handle of the sword faced the knight, and the blade pointed to the center of the Round Table. This act was a reminder to every knight to communicate in a way that values all ideas and persons at the table. When a knight felt offended, instead of raising the sword in battle, the knight would raise the sword as a sign that communication was somehow not as open as it needed to be."

Jim said, "So, the sword kept everyone mindful of the bloody past when communication was not effective. And it was used in a bloodless way to make sure everyone felt they were heard, right?"

"Absolutely, Jim. All ideas had to be heard and valued as worthy of consideration and discussion," said Arthur. "Without openness, we would be less effective at building Camelot."

Jim then interjected, "Old habits die hard for many people, Your Majesty. For your knights, battle was a way of life. In my time, battles between my knights in Marketing and R&D are a way of life too. I would like to change that.

"How did you get your knights to stop the battles and start communicating? How did you create a place where communication at the Round Table was no longer interrupted by unproductive or unfounded fighting?"

Arthur responded, "You are right that old habits die hard, Jim. To survive, knights must be technically excellent in battle. Knights are groomed for battle from the time they are small children.

"In the peace of the Round Table, the knights missed the physical exhilaration of being fit for battle. There was only so much openness they could handle.

"So, they chose to create contests we called the joust. The joust gave the knights an opportunity to prove their ability in battle. It gave them a chance to hone their skills and prove their expertise in front of each other and the world. And most important of all, it gave them a chance to learn from each other and create new ways to improve their abilities as Knights of the Round Table."

Jim remembered seeing a joust at the Renaissance Festival the previous summer in Atlanta. One of the events had two knights in full battle armor. Mounted on horses galloping at partial speed, the knights charged each other holding the weapon that reminded Jim of a telephone pole. Both knights got knocked off their horses, and one of them was hurt enough to be carted away in an ambulance.

Jim said, "Your Majesty, jousts are dangerous! You say the knights jousted for practice?"

Arthur responded, "Yes, Jim. Jousts *are* dangerous. But the knights needed a place to size up each other's skills and learn more about each other. In battles, knights tried to kill each other and increase their possessions. In contrast, jousts held at Camelot let knights learn new skills and techniques from each other. It gave them an effective way to exchange a lot of information."

One of the problems on Jim's team was that the team members didn't know much about each other, technically *or* non-technically. Without the ease of a coffee break, they had little informal opportunity to collaborate informally or to ask each other for suggestions. They knew little of each other's successes in their own battles for survival amidst so much downsizing.

Jim felt if the team members *did* have this knowledge, they would communicate better across distance. So, Jim made a mental note to find a way to establish an electronic joust for his own team. He didn't need the emphasis on battle that Arthur's team had. But Jim did feel a need to set up a way for the people to learn more about each other. Perhaps an electronic yearbook that gives each team member's accomplishments, backgrounds, and favorite types of work would help.

Jim also thought to establish an informal, non-agenda *audioconference meeting* he would call the *Friday Joust*, to help the team bring problems to the table for the others to suggest solutions. Jim made a mental note to talk about this with his team.

Jim then asked, "How did the joust help improve communication at the Round Table, Sire?"

Arthur responded, "The joust was an outlet that let the knights find common interests and experiences. They shared techniques and formed partnerships. The friendships that were born in those partnerships added to the richness and productivity of Camelot. It allowed me to focus on moving battles away from the Round Table, so that I could create the level of openness that was needed to build Camelot."

Arthur and Jim's conversation was interrupted by the ringing of the cellular phone in Jim's car. Before he picked up the telephone handset, Jim commented, "Here is another new technology you'll like, Your Majesty. It's called a cellular telephone."

Arthur noticed Jim use another word with the prefix *tele*. A lot of words in Jim's world began with *tele*. Arthur wanted to understand the word better. He made a mental note to talk with Jim about that word later. Right now, though, he just watched Jim respond to the ringing noise.

Jim excused himself, picked up the receiver, and answered the call. It was Mauro, the team member from Italy. Jim greeted Mauro with a friendly *Buon Giorno! Come sta, signore?* Then he quickly asked Mauro if it would be OK to use the speakerphone. When Mauro said yes, Jim placed the handset back in the carrier and continued the conversation so Arthur could hear.

Mauro had an idea he wanted to run by Jim briefly on the phone. No sooner did Mauro present the idea, when Jim responded, "I'm glad you shared the idea, Mauro, but we already considered that." Jim thought he saw Arthur grimace as he heard Jim speak those words to Mauro. Shortly afterward, the conversation was ended, with Jim thanking Mauro for his call. He closed with a friendly *arrivederci!* and hung up.

Jim said, "That was Mauro, Sire. He is a member of the project team. He lives in Rome. Sometimes he travels to Atlanta. We meet mostly, however, by telephone. Telephone lets me hear his voice. Sometimes we meet by video teleconference which lets me see him on a television monitor. I will show you these technologies some time. Whenever I need to meet with anyone on my project team, telecommunications technology is there to help us communicate together."

Jim's description of telecommunications made a word pop into Arthur's mind. With Arthur's quick wit, the king said to Jim, "So you don't just meet your knights at the Round Table. You meet them at the *Tele*-Round Table!"

Jim immediately smiled, obviously pleased with the idea. "Yes, Your Majesty, I like that! The *Tele*-Round Table! The Tele-Round Table for my team is the world itself!"

Jim's mind once again pictured Arthur's magnificent Round Table. Just like the special effects Industrial Light and Magic brought to the movie *Terminator 2*, Jim saw Arthur's Round Table transform into its more modern form. The transformation began with a large flat table with knights in full battle armor seated around it. It ended with a 3-dimensional globe that looked like a hologram. Jim's knights, wearing modern, comfortable clothes, were seated around it. A variety of familiar technologies connected them.

Arthur smiled, pleased with his creativity in finding a name for a symbol of communication in Jim's high-tech era. Then Arthur asked, "When people sit at your Tele-Round Table, Jim, do they have the right to be heard, no matter where at the table they sit?"

"Of course, Your Majesty. I always listen to their ideas."

"If you were Mauro, would you feel your ideas were heard at the Tele-Round Table just a few moments ago?"

"Well, yes, I listened to him. I didn't tell him that I knew the group that was working on that problem was close to making a decision. I knew they were leaning in a different direction than the one Mauro suggested. I didn't want to bog the conversation down in the details. So I just gave him feedback that I didn't think the idea would fly.

Should I have handled this situation differently, Your Majesty?"

Arthur responded, "Your knights do not want an *answer* to their ideas. Mauro called you because he trusts you as leader to listen. He trusts you to champion his idea. He expects that whatever he brings to your Tele-Round Table will be acted upon."

Almost indignantly, Jim stated, "I can't *champion* ideas that I don't think will work, Your Majesty. Mauro didn't have all the facts."

Arthur said, "Championing an idea does not mean you fight the battle *for* the knight. Your role as leader is to give the knight the information he needs to do battle himself. In his isolation, he won't have all the facts you do. And you don't have all of his. He trusts you to supply those perspectives or to act on his idea. If you don't, you break trust.

"Mauro needed to know the details that you knew but did not share. Then he could make the decision not to battle for the idea, or be armed to carry the idea further. He did not want action on his battle to end with you. He wanted his suggestion to you at the Tele-Round Table to be a *beginning*.

"If you champion his idea, you will build trust. That knight will work even harder for you, no matter if he is in his castle or in Camelot. If you do not champion his idea, he will feel powerless. Then he will go elsewhere where he can feel more power. He'll retreat to his castle to possibly undermine yours."

A light went on in Jim's head. Suddenly Jim saw all of

the times he cut off ideas without realizing it. At the Tele-Round Table, one of Jim's most important leadership tasks was to build trust that communication is open. Now he could see he had some real work to do.

"What I hear you saying, Sire, is that I must be open and responsive to ideas my knights bring to me at the Tele-Round Table. My team trusts that I am fair and open. They trust I will support them. They trust their idea will be considered fairly. If I arbitrarily dismiss their idea, I break trust."

"Yes, Jim, *every idea presented at the Tele-Round Table must be handled in a way that seems fair to the knight who offered it*," responded Arthur.

Jim was pulling into the parking lot at the office. He was due at a meeting and reluctantly knew he had to sign off shortly with Arthur.

Jim, reflecting on Arthur's suggestion about openness at the Round Table, said, "I will call Mauro back, Your Majesty, to find out more about his idea and to give him more information from my perspective.

"I've always felt that, as leader, I had to have all the answers. I always thought making decisions was part of my job. That's one reason why I responded to Mauro so quickly.

"You've helped me see that in the isolation of distance, I can't see what Mauro sees. He can't see what I see. Neither of us has all the information we need to make an effective decision. Therefore, openness is critical.

"I will be a lot more attentive to being open, as you suggest. I guess I always thought openness was just being friendly or saying a few words in someone else's language. You've helped me understand, though, that *real* openness is a whole lot more than talking in a friendly way. Real openness creates an understanding that helps us arrive at a better decision together."

Arthur nodded his head in agreement. "Yes, Jim. Openness helps both of you see what distance prevents you from seeing. And it builds commitment, too, which is a terrific reward for communicating well."

Jim had one more brief topic to cover before signing off with Arthur. "Sire, bringing the Knights of the Round Table to Camelot for meetings must have taken a lot of effort and money. The money I have available for travel was just slashed by 25 percent. I don't know how important travel is to the trust my team must develop."

Arthur responded, *"Travel to Camelot for our first meeting was the most expensive, yet the most important, investment I made.* Without the chance to meet each other face to face at first, the knights had no trust. Without trust, Camelot would have failed.

"That first meeting let the knights find common ground to develop relationships. It let them share ideas about what Camelot should look like. It helped to crystallize the result we could create together, but not separately. As the knights talked and shared, the picture of Camelot became very clear and exciting to every knight.

"Quite frankly, Jim, if I had not invested in bringing the knights to Camelot at the beginning, we could never have built such a wonderful place. The dream of Camelot would

have existed only in my mind, never to have been enjoyed by anyone except me."

That did it! Jim was going to march into his boss's office and fight to keep his travel budget at last year's level. Jim felt the lack of travel was hurting his team. Some of the people traveled to see some of the others, but the entire team had not met in one location face to face. Jim could see that the only communication that was happening across distance was between people who met one another in person earlier.

Jim reluctantly had to say good-bye to Arthur. Jim grabbed his briefcase, got out of the car, and locked the door.

As Jim walked toward the office door, he laughed out loud when he thought of how he would answer the one question he knew his boss would surely ask: What makes you so convinced that travel is important?

"Because King Arthur said I needed it for the Knights of my Tele-Round Table!"

Camelot

fter work four days later, Jim drove to the Evergreen Conference Center. He made an appearance at a company barbecue that was being held on one of the center's expansive patios. His real reason for attending, however, was to talk informally with his boss. At Jim's request, Jim's boss committed a chunk of money to fund a one-site meeting of the worldwide project team. Jim spent about a half an hour thanking his boss for the support and talking about some of his plans for it.

After a few other obligatory hellos, Jim sneaked down to the athletic center and changed into his jogging clothes. He packed a small mirror, the magic coin, and his car keys into a small waist pack. And then he jogged out of the front door of the center.

Jim was familiar with the jogging route between the

center and Stone Mountain. It was one of his favorite trails, and he had taken it several times. He always enjoyed being surrounded by the towering trees, which made him feel humble, yet connected to nature. Several years ago, Jim found an almost hidden trailhead that led him to a secluded clearing deeper in the woods. Jim enjoyed the isolation of that part of the woods. He would frequently jog there and spend an entire day reading, never encountering any other human being but himself. Today, he would take Arthur there.

As soon as he arrived at the clearing, Jim found a rock on which he could place the mirror. Thick, soft grass that encircled the rock invited Jim to sit and enjoy the coolness and quiet of the remaining daylight. Jim took the mirror out of the waist pack. He placed it on the rock and then used the coin to connect with Arthur.

The scene behind Arthur had changed from the last two times they visited. Through the mirror, in a clearing on the top of one of the hills in the rolling countryside stood the castle at Camelot. Camelot was much closer, and Jim could see the castle in much more detail.

Camelot sat at the crest of a beautiful rolling hill. Three gray spires reached up to the heavens, as if to touch the low gray clouds that blanketed the sky. The castle had no windows, except for one slit at the top of the tallest tower.

At the moment, the castle seemed to have no life at all. No horses were entering or leaving the main gate to the castle. No people were moving inside or outside of it.

Except for the rain, the birds, and Arthur, the scene in Arthur's time had no life at all.

"My Liege, I see a beautiful castle in the background over your shoulder. Is it Camelot?" asked Jim.

Jim could hear the light rainfall tapping lightly against the leaves of Arthur's world. "Yes," said Arthur, "it is the castle at Camelot."

Arthur turned and looked at the castle. He stared at it for a moment, his mind filled with other moments, other times, when Camelot was growing and flowering like a rose in spring. In the same flash, Arthur remembered when Camelot was nothing more than a dream. He remembered when the meadow was just a meadow, not a meadow capped with a dream come true.

The pain and joy in Arthur's heart were both reflected in his face as he turned back toward Jim. Arthur spoke. "You asked me earlier today what pulled the knights together across distance, Jim. The Round Table was one critical element. But it was only part of the picture."

Arthur's voice then slowed on his next sentence. Every word reflected his passion for all the meaning he felt inside. "The dream of Camelot was another."

Then Arthur's voice resumed its normal rhythm. "Both the Round Table and the dream of Camelot were needed to unite the knights as one, Jim. One could not have existed without the other."

Suddenly, Arthur's attention shifted to Jim. Arthur was curious how Jim saw the castle. So he asked, "When you look at this castle, Jim, what do you see?"

Jim responded. "I see a beautiful castle, Your Majesty. It is very large and looks like many people could have lived in it. It must have taken many people with fine skills to build it. It looks like it must have had a gorgeous view of England's countryside. If war were to occur, it looks as if it would have given the people inside good protection from enemies, Sire," said Jim as honestly as he could reply to his mentor.

Arthur sat quietly for a moment, processing all of the feelings deep inside. The words Jim used to describe Camelot were not at all what Arthur would have chosen.

Finally, Arthur spoke. "It is amazing how differently we view the same object, Jim. I understand your view, and everything you have said is correct. But one key element is missing, friend. I and all who live in my time have seen a part of Camelot that you are unable to see. That key element is what gave Camelot its life. It is also a critical element that made people from every part of England want to take part in nourishing its fruitful growth."

Jim was puzzled. Arthur's words reflected a whole world of meaning that was yet unsaid to Jim. "I do not understand, Sire. *What* gave Camelot its life?" asked Jim.

Arthur replied, "To me, your words describe a physical structure, an object—which the castle at Camelot is. The *real* Camelot, though, my friend, has nothing to do with any physical object or task. Instead, it has everything to do with the human spirit. It was the vision of Camelot that tapped into the human spirit that gave Camelot life."

Arthur sat down and continued his story. "The *real* Camelot, Jim, is a warm and wonderful place where humankind creates something wonderful for itself. It is a place that unleashes human potential to create something new and different and important together. It is a giant leap forward from where we have been, and it is a leap that everyone wants to make.

"So, when *I* look at the castle at Camelot, I see the human piece, not the bricks and mortar. It was the *human* piece—the human spirit—that created it, built it, and made it great. It was the *human* piece that linked the knights from the farthest reaches of the land. It was the *human* piece that motivated the knights during the months they worked separately from their individual castles. Tragically, it is the *human* piece that now is missing that makes the castle look so barren and still. It is the missing human spirit that takes away Camelot's life."

Even in his youth, when listening to the legend of King Arthur, Jim always thought of Camelot as just a castle, a building. He had never even considered that emotion would be so much a part of its creation. Now, today, he was genuinely surprised at the level of feeling Arthur attached to Camelot.

All of these thoughts prompted Jim to ask, "In the year 2000, Your Majesty, business is *business*. My project plan has a list of goals, tasks, and deadlines. It is very uncomfortable for me, and most people I know to bring emotions into the business of work. I am curious to understand more about the emotional part of Camelot's creation."

Arthur responded, "In my time, Jim, there are many people who can design and build very beautiful castles.

They could build very strong fortresses to seal off vandals and outsiders.

"Were Camelot just a structure—a task to be done—it would have been just any other castle on a hilltop. It would have been a place built for the king's pleasure and no one else's.

"Thank heavens Camelot was not such a hollow place. Camelot attracted the best minds, creativity, and ideas of knights throughout the land. From coast to coast, people joined together, not to build a building, but to do something extraordinary together.

"Camelot had a good plan, Jim. It attracted the best people throughout all of England. The factor that drove the knights to excellence, though, was not the plan alone. It was the people. From the first stone laid for its foundation, Camelot was built *from* heart, *with* heart."

Jim spoke. "When I think of knights, I think of brave men who do not act from their hearts. I am so surprised to hear you speak of how important the human element apparently was to you and to your knights, Your Majesty."

Arthur responded, "I used to think that knights had no emotions, too, Jim. For years, they fought each other with no other intent than to kill—or survive. I was wrong. I began to realize my faulty assumption when I had to win the support of Sir Dinadan, the first knight to defy me as the new King of England.

"When I became King, only the people who were present on the field where I pulled Excalibur out of the rock gave me instant recognition as their king. However, word about it traveled more slowly than I did through some parts of England.

"Three days later, two squires and I were traveling north, when I met Sir Dinadan. He and two squires were traveling in the opposite direction from me, examining his property. Dinadan said I had trespassed on his land. Because in those days might *was* right, he was forced to challenge my intrusion in battle. He didn't believe I was king. Besides that, he said he had never sworn allegiance to *any* king, so it wouldn't have made any difference even if I were.

"I didn't want to do battle, but Dinadan wouldn't back down. Honor dictated that I choose the battle instrument, so I selected the joust. In the first pass, we both knocked each other off our horses. The impact was so hard, both of the jousting poles were broken.

"Chivalry then dictated that he follow my lead in selecting the next instrument. I pulled the Sword Excalibur from my horse's saddle. He matched my selection. Then we battled with swords for only moments when I knocked him to the ground. I walked over to Dinadan with Excalibur still in hand, and I stood tall above his prone, battle-wounded body.

"Earlier in the battle, I had knocked off the face shield of Dinadan's helmet, which now exposed his angry face. As he now spoke, his lips were tight, exposing his wrath with his clenched teeth. With an incensed tone of voice, Dinadan shouted his command to me. 'Kill me, *supposed king,* and do it swiftly! Thrust your sword through my throat. I will not flinch or move, so I hold my honor to my dying breath.'

"I stood there for a moment. My standing body towered over his horizontal one like a castle turret over a fallen tree. My heavy boot clamped the knight's shoulder to the ground as I held Excalibur's pointed edge at the hollow of his throat.

" 'What is your name, knight?' I asked.

" 'Sir Dinadan. Sir Dinadan of Darby. Now that you know my name, stranger, wait no longer. I am ready to die! I am weary of a life of killing so many others. It is *this* life I choose to end so I can be more productive in heaven. *I want to die with honor.*'

"This conversation repeated itself several more times, while I stood above him trying to decide what to do. Do I do what kings before me did and kill the victim? Or do I act differently?

"I remember breathing so hard and feeling such power and such pain all at once. I stared at his eyes. But for some reason, I was too paralyzed to plunge the sword through his neck exactly as the defeated knight told me to do.

"Dinadan's eyes bid me to wait no longer. His trembling body impatiently waited for the final strike from his victor that would send him to eternity. After a moment more of frozen stillness that shielded all the thoughts whirling through my mind, I finally responded to my battle partner. 'No!'

"Dinadan was furious. '*No!* How can you say *no!*

Chivalry dictates that you destroy me!' Dinadan shouted, outraged by the dilemma that I, a stranger, cast him into.

"I removed my foot from Dinadan's shoulder and pulled Excalibur back to my side. With one swift motion, I threw back the face mask of my own helmet so he could see my face while I spoke.

"I then looked Dinadan straight in the eye, and said, 'Death does no honor, Dinadan. Destruction bears no reward. I want you to join me, Sir Dinadan. I want you to be productive with me in changing this desperate life! I want you to join me in building a new world of peace and productivity in Camelot. Camelot will act as a symbol to usher in a new era under me, your new king—King Arthur of Camelot.'

"Dinadan was confused. He half sat up. He leaned the upper half of his body on his elbows. His eyes suddenly recognized the Sword Excalibur, which Dinadan himself had failed to remove from the rock some months earlier. Dinadan knew Excalibur could only be removed from the rock by a great king! Dinadan now knew his victor was, in fact, me, the *King of England!*

"As rapidly as a knight can move in a heavy suit of armor, Dinadan tried to get on his knees, so he could bow to his king. But like a turtle on its back, all Dinadan could do was roll back and forth. I extended my hand and knew, when he took it, that he would join me.

"Now, Jim, do you think a knight's life is free of emotion?" asked Arthur.

Jim responded, "No, Your Majesty. Your story helps me see that being a knight was a very emotional experience. It went beyond being skilled at swords, knives, and battle axes. There is emotion in the execution of skills on the battlefield. There is emotion in the life or death consequences of battle. There is emotion in the victory and in the defeat. I just never saw it.

"The story you have told me reminds me that the technical knights on my Tele-Round Table have an emotional core, too. There is emotion in reaching technical excellence. There is emotion in being on a winning project. There is emotion if they fail. Even though we don't talk about it in business, as a leader I need to know it's there. And I need to learn how to tap into that emotional base."

Arthur said, "The Knights of the Round Table would never have admitted an emotional link. In fact, it wasn't *knightly* to talk about emotions. The important point, though, Jim, is *emotions are there.* As leader, tapping into the positive side of those emotions can be one of your most powerful links in creating your Camelot.

"My battle to gain Dinadan's commitment to me and to Camelot had another important element, too—involvement. The emotional link can be strengthened and sustained over time by involvement and participation. When I tell you what happened next, you'll see what I mean.

"Dinadan and I made camp together at the base of a rolling meadow peak. We tied the horses to a branch of an old raintree that was so huge it seemed that it could cover a crowd of 300! That night, the sky was crystal clear. Millions of bright stars almost made the night sky as bright as day. The stars were so numerous in some clusters, they seemed to form clouds of their own up high in the universe. Nature is so magnificent!

"The infinite sky reminded the knight and me of the infinite capability of man. Dinadan and I talked for two days about what Camelot should look like and what it shouldn't look like. Before Dinadan, I had a dream of Camelot myself. As we talked, Dinadan's ideas made that dream better and even more exciting. The more he contributed his ideas, the more I saw his commitment toward Camelot grow.

"In that conversation, Dinadan and I didn't describe a castle. We described a symbol of a way of life that was to transcend all of England. And he clearly saw himself as part of that important adventure.

"The reason I tell you this story, Jim, is that Dinadan wanted Camelot to happen too. Our discussions planted the seeds for his personal commitment to making Camelot real. By the end of the two days, our conversations expanded Camelot into a dream that was even more compelling to both of us. Camelot was no longer optional. We *had* to make it happen.

"In order to insure Camelot's success, I knew I had to build a level of commitment in him and other knights that would not need my prodding to continue. *If Camelot was to be successful, his commitment had to be so high that it continued to grow and thrive when he was away from me. That level of commitment has a solid emotional base.* Plain and simple, he had to care enough to keep at it without the influence of the other knights or me who would be distant from him most of the time.

"That meeting occurred nearly twenty years ago right

here in this spot," said Arthur, pointing to the ground just under his feet. He twisted his upper torso to face the castle and said, "Just look over there behind me. That structure is the embodiment of many of the concepts Dinadan and I talked about two decades ago."

The story sent a chill up Jim's spine. In some ways, he wished he could have been Sir Dinadan, because Jim knew he would have enjoyed working with his regal friend. When Arthur paused, Jim asked, "Your Majesty, so you, alone, did not create Camelot?"

"Oh, no, Jim. I had an idea for Camelot. I was committed to making it happen. But I did not have all the answers. Nor did I know all the questions that needed to be asked. It was clear I couldn't create Camelot alone.

"My discussion with Dinadan taught me that if I wanted to build commitment for other knights, they also had to be a part of its creation. I now knew the way to unite the knights with one another, with me, and with Camelot. If a knight felt *personally* passionate about the future we would create together, I would have his commitment, near or far from me."

Jim couldn't believe what he had heard. Arthur was telling him to have a *vision*! Right now at work, Jim was on *vision overload,* and so was everyone else on his team. Jim knew of eight different visions in his company, and he saw very little impact of vision on performance.

"Sire, the term people use in my time for the picture you describe is vision. I have got to say honestly that I have a hard time buying into the concept. It just doesn't work. In my business, we go through all kinds of processes to create a vision. When the process is over, the vision sits in the closet unused. Worse yet, it's misused or misunderstood.

"In fact, Your Majesty, we're almost in a time of vision backlash. Although some people believe in visions, an increasing number no longer do."

Arthur's surprise at Jim's comment was reflected in his face. "Visions in your day are not used? Maybe that's the difference, my friend. For the Knights of the Round Table, the vision was a key driver that was alive every day in every part of the country," replied Arthur.

"In fact, Jim, I can say with a high degree of confidence that *without the vision, Camelot would never have been created. Like my predecessors, I, too, would have failed in leading across distance.*"

"Why are you saying that vision is so critical, My Liege?" asked Jim.

Arthur responded. "Pretend you are me, Jim. You want to create a Camelot with people in your own castle. How would you keep everyone motivated?"

Jim thought for a moment, and then replied, "As leader, I would create trust in Camelot by talking a lot about it. I would wander around and become a physical symbol of commitment to making the vision happen. Because everyone is in the castle, I and everyone can keep tabs on progress. I and everyone would be easily accessible. I and everyone can motive each other and help each other along."

Arthur then said, "Let's adjust the situation a little.

This time, you want to create a Camelot with people from different castles. How do you keep everyone motivated?"

Jim had a difficult time coming up with an answer. He finally said, "It would be tougher, Your Majesty. I could talk about it when people visited with me. But if they work mostly away from me, I will have few opportunities to talk. It would be difficult to wander around enough, too. If there were many locations, it just takes too much time and money to travel. The knights would have limited opportunities to motivate each other. It takes a lot of effort for them to help each other along across distance."

Jim paused for a moment and then added one more thought. "If they have a history of mistrust, all of this, as difficult as it is now, becomes even more difficult."

Arthur then said, "So, Jim, people who work in one castle get their motivation from a physical presence or closeness to one another. People who work from a distance, for the most part, lack a physical presence on a daily basis. They need a powerful dynamic to pull them together."

Arthur now had piqued Jim's interest. "What is the dynamic that united the Knights of the Round Table, Sire?" asked Jim.

"The knights were bonded in two ways, Jim. The first was an emotional bond. Camelot had to be a concept each and every knight embraced and cared very deeply about. The idea of Camelot had to bond them on a very personal, even intimate level. *The bond came from their involvement in defining what Camelot would look like, and then taking a leadership role in making part of it happen.*

"When knights are apart from their king, they will

only do those things that are a priority to them personally. *They won't do what the king thinks is important. They will only do what they find important in their everyday world.*

"The second link was an intellectual link. Every knight shared the same clear description of what Camelot looks like. When we first met at the Round Table, the knights spent days defining *exactly* what Camelot was to be. We wrote down the key parts of Camelot agreed on by everyone at the Round Table."

Jim then said, "So, Sire, let me translate what you've just said to apply to my team. The people on my team work in separate locations. In order to keep them all headed in the same direction when they are distant, I need to align them in two ways. One way is intellectual. Everyone needs clear agreement on what we are creating together. The second way is emotional. Everyone needs to care on a personal level that the worldwide task is worthwhile. Is that right?"

"Yes, Jim, you are right. But we are still not done with how to keep the people and the activity aligned, so you get the result you want across distance. There is one more important step," said Arthur.

The king continued, "You need a daily decision tool. Let me tell you about how the daily decision tool helps.

"At the Round Table, we decided that *we needed a question or a statement we could ask ourselves every day that would align us in our work throughout the land. If we could respond in the affirmative to the daily decision tool, we were aligned from every part of the country.*"

Jim was confused. He had no idea, on a project as complex as building Camelot, what one question would align the people to the vision. "What was the decision tool for the Knights of the Round Table, Your Majesty?"

"*Might for right*, Jim," responded Arthur.

The lights went on in Jim's head. "I know the phrase, 'might for right,' Sire. It's in the legend! You changed it from might *is* right to might *for* right!"

Arthur was delighted. "Yes, Jim! Might *for* right became our new battle cry. We used it to change *de*structive battle into *con*structive battle. Each day, as each knight did his work to build Camelot, he could ask himself, 'Did I use might *for* right?' If he did, he knew he did his job well. He could pat himself on the back, and he could tell me and others about it. If he did not, he knew to stop doing whatever he was doing. He knew to change his actions or ask for help from me or other knights."

Jim thought about how some teams created their vision and mission statements. In his company, it almost seemed the visions were created as an end, not a means to an end. He recalled one vision statement that failed. It stated, "To deliver outstanding service from the customer's perspective." The leadership team that created it went through the process, but they didn't really embrace the concept. No one in the service organization knew the words. Management never talked about it. So, the front-line service reps continued to deliver service they wanted to give, rather than what the customer wanted.

Jim now saw that the vision statement could function as a decision tool. Front-line service providers could use those words to judge their personal interaction with customers. Management could use those words in coaching customer service agents. They could use those words as part of the decision process to change outdated processes and procedures. They could structure reward and incentive programs around it. They could make those words a rallying cry to give one clear direction for people at all service locations. In short, everyone can make decisions by the decision tool.

Jim's mind began to see a shift in his role as leader. He knew he held the key responsibility for effective decisions. It was clear, though, he couldn't be present for all decisions worldwide, nor did he want to be. Many more decisions would have to be made than he could personally handle.

Besides that, people always complained how difficult it was to reach one another spontaneously across distance. It seemed that now the firm had voice mail, no one was at his or her desk anymore! The decision tool would let each of his distant team members make *effective* decisions on a daily basis, especially if they couldn't get a response in time.

Jim wasn't sure if he was seeing what Arthur wanted him to see. So he asked, "I see that you have structured the intellectual link, the emotional link, and the decision tool to touch the knight on a very individual and personal level. Was that your leadership strategy, Sire?"

Arthur responded, "Yes, Jim. All of these techniques focus every knight, in every castle, in every part of the country, to aim for the same objective. *It is critically important that you, as leader, keep these bonds in the daily language and thought of every knight of your Tele-Round Table, near and far.* We'll talk more about how I did that in another of our talks later. Does that sound all right, Jim?"

Jim agreed. Darkness was rapidly approaching in Atlanta. Jim knew that he would have a difficult time finding his way out of the forest in the dark if he didn't leave soon.

Before the meeting ended, Arthur made one more point. "Emotional connections can be very uncomfortable for some people, Jim. The emotional connection I spoke to you about today is not necessarily that the knights gathered to talk about very personal matters. Quite the contrary.

"The emotional link centered around what Camelot *represented*. The knights felt important by being involved in creating it. They had a respectful relationship with me that grew each time I supported them and listened to them."

Jim interjected, "So the emotions were on an internal level. It wasn't people gushing out a lot of personal information about each other. Instead, it was more about finding a way to hook into the emotional part of each person to secure their commitment to Camelot."

Arthur said, "Exactly."

Arthur and Jim set a time to meet the next day. They wished each other well, and said good-bye.

As Jim jogged out of the clearing, he replayed parts of the conversation with Arthur over again in his head.

Jim ended the day a changed leader. For the first time in his life, he felt comfortable with the emotional connection Arthur described. Jim was comfortable creating an intellectual link, an emotional link, and a decision tool to keep the team moving forward in one direction, worldwide.

Jim began to formulate a plan to bring his team together for a single-site meeting to create these important links.

Lancelot

aturday morning, Jim caught a flight to Washington, D.C. He decided to treat himself to a weekend in one of his favorite places in the United States—the nation's capital. Jim was registered to attend a three-day leadership conference there, beginning the following Monday.

For the weekend, holding a small mirror in his hand, Jim took Arthur on a sightseeing tour. Arthur was in awe as Jim showed him the Lincoln Memorial, the Washington Monument, the Capitol Building, and the Supreme Court. Arthur was engrossed as Jim related the legends and history affixed to these landmark symbols of his nation's greatness.

Then Jim walked across the greens and sat on a park bench opposite the White House. The home of the president stood like a monument on its perfectly manicured grounds. Jim gave Arthur some perspective of the important office of president. Arthur was delighted to learn that one U.S. president, President Kennedy, had his term dubbed as Camelot.

A little later, Jim rambled over to the Vietnam Memorial. Both Arthur and Jim were speechless at The Wall. The 58,000 names that covered the black wall were overwhelming. Arthur commented, "What kind of wars do you have that so many would die?" Each name was a loved one lost in the name of war. Jim was still struggling with some of his feelings about the war in Vietnam. Knowing the pain of battle, Arthur found himself fighting back emotion, too, at the massive display of the bitter, tragic loss of life.

On Sunday, Jim and Arthur spent the day wandering through the aerospace exhibit in one of the Smithsonian's fabulous museums. Jim positioned the mirror so Arthur could see all of the displays and the video presentations. Arthur was speechless after watching a videotape of Armstrong's "one small step for a man, one giant leap for mankind" first steps on the moon. Arthur thought of the night he and Dinadan sat under the raintree and talked of no limits. Arthur never imagined man would land on the moon—ever!

Arthur enjoyed the tour so much Jim wished he could have shown Arthur the art, architecture, and beauty of Europe, the Far East, and other beautiful countries around the world.

Before Jim knew it, Monday had arrived. He attended

his conference, but learned little new information to help him lead across distance. All he heard was the same old stuff that assumed the people working on the project were physically co-located. Jim's reality was they weren't.

At the conference, Jim picked up a few new ideas. But the most relevant leadership ideas came from his sessions with his royal mentor, King Arthur. Jim was using Arthur's ideas every day, and he was getting results.

By the following Thursday, Jim was back in Atlanta. Jim had begun to initiate Arthur's suggestions, but knew he still needed more help. He wanted Arthur to be able to see more details of his daily interactions with his team.

At work, Jim couldn't carry around a compact mirror all day so Arthur could travel more easily with him, as in D.C. Instead, Jim had to find an inconspicuous way to create a communication window in some key locations that he used frequently when in the building. He finally thought of a way. He decided to hang mirrors on three strategic walls at work.

On Monday, Jim got to work by 6:15 A.M. to hang the mirrors before anyone arrived at work. He put one in the video conference meeting room and one in his office.

He put the hook for the third mirror by the coffee pot, so Arthur could witness the all-American coffee break. As Jim was about to hang the mirror on it, though, he heard the latch on the door next to the area click. With a force that seemed as strong as a gorilla's, the door exploded open.

Jim felt like a kid with a hand in the cookie jar! Even though he had done nothing wrong by installing the mirrors, he still felt guilty. Jim hoped the person who was about to walk through the door was no one he knew. As it turned out, though, it was the person he knew best in the company, Robert.

Jim's tense voice said, "Oh, it's only you, Robert!" Robert, Jim's first-hand man and project teammate, had arrived early that day, too. Robert was 6′2″, weighed about 240 pounds, and used to be a star linebacker in college at Michigan State. Robert's German ancestry helped him be aggressive, meticulous, and win-oriented in business. These qualities, combined with Robert's lively sense of humor, were the qualities Jim liked best about his number one teammate.

Robert's eyes looked first at Jim and then at the mirror. Robert's face did not conceal his initial reaction to wonder why Jim was hanging a mirror by the coffee pot. With his quick wit, Robert decided to tease Jim. *"Ach die lieber!* Are you trying to blind me this morning, Jim? Now we'll have *two* reflections while we're here at the coffee pot. The mirror and your head!" said Robert, as he looked in the mirror to straighten his tie.

Jim's heart was pounding so loudly he wondered if Robert could see it pumping through the shirt. He waited for Robert to reflexively shout when he saw King Arthur looking at him. But Robert didn't flinch. He looked in the mirror that Jim held, and then straightened his tie. Amazingly, Robert couldn't see Arthur. Robert only saw himself.

Jim laughed at Robert's joke and howled inside at this comical situation! Jim decided to make light of Robert's morning joke. "Just adding more glow to your morning, Robert!"

Robert knew he made a funny comment. He was puzzled, though, why Jim continued to laugh for some time afterward. When the laughter subsided, he saw Jim glance briefly into the mirror, only to break out in laughter again.

Robert thought Jim was *losing it*. Too much stress! Robert couldn't see Arthur doubled over in laughter. But Jim did. The look on Robert's face expressed some confusion as to what had sparked this atypical behavior. Jim tried to suppress the laugh, but his red face and bulging eyes looked like an overblown balloon about to pop.

Trying to suppress another wave of laughter, Jim quickly hung the mirror on the hook he had installed seconds earlier. He immediately poured a cup of coffee for both of them, and motioned for Robert to join him in a walk down the hall to their desks. Jim tried to divert Robert's attention to other matters by changing the topic to football. He asked in footballeze, "What about those Falcons, eh? Did ya' see the game last night?"

Jim had come to rely a great deal on Robert as a professional associate and a good friend. They worked very closely together on the project, and they got along well. Jim tended to rely more on Robert than on any of the other team members. Robert was convenient and accessible on a moment's notice, and he enjoyed every challenge Jim threw his way. Jim trusted Robert implicitly. The respect was mutual.

They also belonged to the same athletic club and the same company baseball league. They enjoyed the same types of interests, and got along very well together. Over the last two months, they found themselves doing more socially together after work and on the weekends, as well. During Jim's divorce a year earlier, Robert gave Jim tremendous support. Robert even fixed Jim up with a couple of blind dates, to help get him back into circulation again.

Jim didn't have social opportunities to work with other team members at a distance. When Jim traveled, he usually flew in, met, and left. He did not want to impose on the personal lives of his distant teammates. So he typically did not schedule dinners or other social activities when he visited those off-site. If someone requested that he join them for dinner, he did. But Jim never initiated it with any of them out of respect for their private lives away from work. He did not yet know it was a mistake for him to make that choice, instead of letting the off-site team members choose.

One other team member, Al, worked on-site in Atlanta. Al was on the fourth floor, though, whereas Jim and Robert were on the twentieth. One day Jim realized he communicated more with the team members in Canada than Al on the fourth floor. Robert, on the other hand, was right outside Jim's door. They communicated all the time.

Jim had several meetings today, all of which Arthur was able to see. The day began with an 11 A.M. E.S.T. video conference meeting with the European team members. All of the Denver team members flew to Atlanta for the meeting. The meeting had to wait for Mark, the supplier in San Diego, to arrive at work at 8:00 California time. Mark was linked in by telephone. Eric and Deiter traveled to Mauro's video conference room to meet at 7 P.M. Rome time.

The meeting did not go as well as Jim would have liked. When the meeting started, Jim referred to the agenda. The European group said they had not received theirs. Mark, the supplier, didn't get one either. "You received the handout materials, didn't you?" asked Jim. No, no one outside of Atlanta got those either. So in a flurry of activity over the next fifteen minutes, copies were quickly faxed.

Although Al was in the room, Jim and Robert did most of the talking during the meeting. Outside of that, some comments were directed to Jim. But no one in Europe directed a question to anyone else in Atlanta but Jim. In fact, they hardly said anything at all.

During the meeting, no one paid any attention to Mark, the supplier, who was linked in by phone. He was transparent, as if he didn't exist at all in the group. Four times during the meeting, Mark asked the people in the Atlanta location to speak more directly into the microphone. No one paid any attention to his request.

Robert tried to use his quick wit to lighten up the meeting. He said a few funny comments that only the Atlanta people heard clearly and responded to. When the European partners did not laugh, Robert just thought they didn't understand the joke.

Arthur noticed the team did accomplish some business. It was apparent, though, that Jim seemed uncomfortable.

After the meeting, Arthur listened to a call Jim received from Eric. Eric complained he felt like a second class citizen. "How else can I feel when we aren't even important enough to get basic materials for a meeting I just spent several hours of my time to travel to Rome to attend!" he said angrily. Eric continued to complain that this was the fifth meeting he attended for this project that was scheduled outside his normal work day in Europe.

Then Eric quipped, "Why don't you and Robert have the meeting, make the decisions, and then just tell us what to do. At least then you won't waste my time!" Jim blew off the comment as another of Eric's temper tantrums.

Later in the day, Jim called Mark, the supplier. Talking through the speakerphone, Mark pelted Jim with angry words about the meeting. Mark said, "Four separate times in the meeting I asked people to speak up. I felt like I was talking into a black hole. No one heard me or acted on my request, *including you, Jim.*"

When Jim apologized, Mark sarcastically said, "No one had to ask Robert to speak up. He spoke just fine." Jim ignored the comment and changed the subject.

Another meeting later in the day with the Denver team members and Jim went poorly, too. They knocked down every thought Robert presented. They laughed only moderately at his jokes. After zinging one comment to Robert, the Denver three gave each other an *in* look that obviously put Robert on the *out* group. They treated Al coldly, too; but mostly they seemed to pick fights with

Robert. Jim dismissed the incident as too childish to even comment on.

Arthur also caught an offhand remark Nicole made. Just after the meeting, Robert made a reference to his racquetball game with Jim the previous week. Nicole said, "We wouldn't know about that. Jim never plays racquetball with us. In fact, when he's in Denver, he never even asks us to join him for dinner."

Jim was put off by Nicole's comment. When he traveled, he never asked out of consideration of *their* time. He wasn't being snobby or unfriendly. Jim knew this outburst was a trust issue, but he really didn't know what to do about it. So he ignored it, at least for the moment.

By the end of the day, Jim knew he was having more than a bad day. Something else was going wrong on the team. Why was everyone picking on Robert? Robert was competent, and everyone knew it. He did a lot of their work, and everyone benefitted from all that he did for the project team. Jim promised himself he would talk about it with Arthur on the way home from work.

On the ride home, Arthur opened the door to the topic by saying, "Jim, I see that you and Robert have become very close friends. Is that right?"

Surprised by Arthur's observation, Jim responded, "Actually, yes, Your Majesty. I've known Robert for about five years, but we only became friends about a year ago. I have come to rely on him and his judgment, especially when something critical comes up. I always know Robert will handle the situation well. I give him a great deal of responsibility because of my trust in him."

Arthur asked a second question, "Do you give the same level of responsibility to the knights who work distantly from you?"

Jim responded, "No, Arthur, I just don't know them or their work well enough. I know they're all competent, but I don't know and trust their competence as much as Robert's. Besides that, Robert is close and convenient, and they're so distant. Sometimes I can't get a response as quickly as I need from the team members who are off-site. So I consult with Robert and don't bother the others.

"Your Majesty, I try to help them by not putting too much pressure on them. I try to help them by not making too many requests. But I sense the meeting today could have gone much better. Did you notice the problem, Sire? Do you have suggestions to help me?"

Arthur said, "I did notice one problem in particular, Jim. I noticed it only because I have been there myself. The same dynamic I saw on your team today happened with my Knights of the Round Table. The problem, Jim, may be rooted in your friendship with Robert."

"Robert?" exclaimed Jim, totally unaware of why Arthur singled out Jim's best friend.

Arthur continued, "You have a friend who is a key knight that works close to you at your castle. Are you familiar with my friend who was the same at my castle?"

Jim knew that answer. "You mean Lancelot, My Liege?"

"Yes, Jim. My friend was Lancelot du Lac. As my friendship with Lance grew, my reliance on him grew.

Over time, my eyes were blind to the jealousy everyone else felt toward my unfaltering trust in him."

"*Jealousy!* Are you saying your knights were jealous of your *friendship* with Lancelot? He was your friend! *Are kings not supposed to have friends?*" asked Jim, sarcastically.

Arthur was afraid Jim would dismiss this issue as trite. So he broached the response carefully, "Leaders *can* have friends, Jim. But a leader runs an enormous risk by befriending some on the team more than others."

Arthur's face could not hide the sadness that gripped his words. He knew he alone was responsible for the fall of Camelot. But he also knew his close friendship with Lancelot was the beginning of the decline.

Jim was curious to know of the great Lancelot from the words of the other in that renowned friendship. Jim asked, "Your friendship with Lancelot is one that is well known in my time, Sire. Please tell me in your own words of your friendship with Lancelot. What was he like?"

Arthur said, "Lancelot was the most remarkable man I've ever known! Not anywhere else on the earth was a human being as bright . . . as witty . . . as committed . . . as positive . . . as loyal. Oh, I could go on for a long time, Jim. *Lance was my best male friend in all of my life.*

"I thirsted to talk with Lance. His mind was so creative. If I asked one question, he came back with a thousand options. In an instant, he could turn a rough, unpolished idea into a beautiful symphony of choices. As if that was not gift enough, he was blessed with a miraculous ability to express his thoughts. He talked with the elegance of a poet, engaging me to explore his every word.

"Outside of myself, I had never seen anyone else embrace life with such vibrance. There was nothing Lance cared only a little about. With every fiber of his being, he loved *all* of his life and *all* of his life's work. He conquered every challenge by mustering phenomenal power from within. *Every* challenge I placed before him he solved so creatively and so well that I thanked God every day that Lance found his way to Camelot."

Jim was engrossed by the way Arthur described his friend. He had never in his life had a male or female friend he could describe so profoundly. Jim asked, "Sire, the legend paints Lancelot as a great man. Your description of him makes me know he was so much more. But something in the legend puzzles me, Your Highness.

"The legend is not as kind to Lancelot as you are with your words now. Why does the legend also portray him as arrogant, self-serving, and in dire need of *humility?* Would you use such negative words to describe Lancelot, too?"

Arthur responded, "No, I would *never* use arrogant or self-serving to describe Lance. Lance was an exceptional man, and he knew it. So did everyone else. Lancelot so greatly stood out from all of the other knights that no one could light a candle next to him. The tasks no one else could do, *he did*.

"He made it so easy for me to rely on his great, great talents! He was so loyal, he made it easy for me to rely on him as a great, great friend. Because he was the only knight who didn't have a castle elsewhere in England, he was easy to find when I needed him. He didn't have a castle other than mine. In seconds, I could tap into his energy, his brilliant thoughts, and his immense personal power to do the impossible.

"I so loved and revered my friend, all I could see was the goodness within him. In time, I relied much more on Lance than any other knight. I trusted his ideas. I gave him more responsibility. I let him prove his excellence over and over again, leaving other knights lacking similar challenges to prove their due.

"When I hear arrogant and self-serving in the legend that survived to your time, I have an idea from whence that view arose.

"When Lance first came to Camelot, the knights resented his pompous words. Lance was passionate about his honor, his life, and his desire to sit as a Knight at the Round Table. Deep in his heart, Lance's soul *was pure*. He was on a life quest to be part of the miracle of Camelot. I could not ever in all of the world have chosen someone I would have wanted more as a brother or trusted friend or partner in making Camelot come true.

"The problem was the knights resented that they were so far away and Lance was so near. They resented my constant reliance on Lance to do the important tasks. They resented my friendship with him and my high regard for all that Lance suggested. They resented the experiences and the time I spent with Lance and not with them."

Jim interjected, "So, are you saying the knights became envious of Lancelot?"

Arthur responded, "Yes, envy is a good word to describe feelings I saw displayed to him—and then to me. The knights were envious because they were isolated from me. They felt isolated from the activity, the decisions, and the challenges that would give them value in their own eyes and mine. They felt like silent partners because so much of what they said fell to my ears, which were deaf to their ideas. They felt they missed opportunities to shine in the eyes of those in their own castles as well.

"The more isolated they felt, the more envious they became. That isolation of the distant knights began Camelot's decline. The knights failed to trust they were united because I didn't foster that trust. I didn't equalize opportunities for each knight to shine among his peers and within his castle. I didn't give them equal chances to feel close to me as their leader.

"When construction of Camelot began, many knights set up campsites for themselves and their servants. They worked from tents spaced across the field just beyond my own entourage of tents that housed me and my servants. The distance of the field kept me from seeing those knights as much as Lancelot, yet we were all at Camelot."

Jim's face turned pale. An imaginary scoreboard popped up in his mind's eye of the people on the project team. Robert 100. Everyone else at a distance 5, including Al on the fourth floor. Jim's imaginary scoreboard exaggerated the true number of times Jim interacted with or relied on Robert versus others on the team. But the numbers were heavily tipped toward his friend, Robert.

Jim then said, "What should I do, Sire? Several of the people on the team have told me they feel isolated. Just as you did with Lancelot, I have relied on Robert both at work and as a friend. Just as your knights resented your closeness with Lancelot, so, too, have some resented my closeness with Robert."

Arthur responded, "Even if Robert and you were *not* close friends, I feel your distant knights would have resented that he was on site with you. Did you notice they picked on Al, too? Even though Al is on a different floor and you don't have the same relationship with him as you do with Robert, they still picked on him. They resented that he was on-site with you, and that sharing the location in Atlanta somehow gave him an advantage with you.

"Lance and I were not good friends at first, but he always did live in my castle. The other knights, even in those early days, watched Lance's every move. If Lance suggested something, they tried to one-up him. If Lance did something, they tried to do something else better. There clearly was a competition for my favor as leader.

"If I place myself in the boots of Sir Sagramore or Sir Dinadan, now I can understand their envy. Both of these knights were also close to me, but their castles were away from mine. They also were friends, but I saw their behavior change when Lancelot came to Camelot. Looking back, I can see so clearly the disappointment on their faces when I gave Lancelot the charge, not them.

"If I place myself in the boots of the other Knights of the Round Table, I know I would have felt genuine frustration. As king, I promised a new and shining Camelot, but didn't give every knight an equal opportunity to shine himself. It was too tough to organize work across distance and monitor progress. I gave most of the glory to my trusted friend, Lancelot."

Jim interjected, "Oh, Your Majesty, I see the parallel between your knights and mine. I don't want to lose my Camelot. We've hardly begun our work. If you had it to do over again, Sire, what would you do differently?"

Arthur answered, "One cannot choose when a truly great friend comes into his life. Although I would have missed one of the finest friendships known to man, I would have chosen not to befriend Lancelot. His friendship gave me what I needed. The envy over that friendship, however, was a major force that destroyed Camelot and the Round Table.

"A remote leader must choose *scrupulous fairness* and *equality of opportunity* when leading people near and far. Your actions must not only be fair, but equally as important, they must be *perceived* as unscrupulously fair by the other knights at a distance.

"Remember, as holder of Excalibur, a king's chief task is to build trust. Every aspect of your leadership must build trust. To do that, make every decision objectively by returning to the decision tool or to agreements made at the original meeting you have with the knights."

Jim asked, "Tell me what *scrupulously fair* would have looked like at the Round Table, Sire."

Arthur responded, "First, every knight gets core information at the same time. Lancelot should not receive more information than the other knights, nor should he receive it sooner. Each knight, whether in Camelot or in his castle, wants to be informed about basic matters of the Round Table. Information makes him feel like he is part of a group. And it keeps him involved."

Jim winced as he remembered that the agendas and meeting materials were not received at all locations before the meeting earlier today. In general, the headquarters site had more information and resources than in the other locations. At the same time, there was unique information in the field. None of those rich sources were being leveraged or shared effectively.

The imbalance definitely put some in the know and others out of the loop. It's no wonder some seemed to drop out in meetings. Jim knew he could only correct this imbalance by structuring a way to share information better.

Arthur proceeded, "Second, every knight has equal input. A knight who lives at or visits my castle has no more influence with me than any other knight who visits here less frequently. I carefully and thoughtfully listen to every idea offered by a knight. I make a point to actively solicit the ideas of knights who are distant from my castle."

Jim was uncomfortable at how much he favored Robert's input over that of the other team members. He could think of only one idea proposed by the Denver team members that was implemented, despite many others that were offered. Bad as that was, it was one better than the number of ideas adopted from the European team members. Maybe that is why the three European team members either sat silently or complained in meetings.

The king continued, "Third, every knight's ideas are weighed against the vision or the decision tool. Decisions are not made on my preference nor on which knight is more convenient. Knights can modify or present ideas as often as they wish, knowing confidently the decision will always be made by our clear, objective decision tool."

Jim could hear all of the times he said to the people on the project team, "We've already considered that," or "We've already made that decision." The *we* was Robert and he, and their decision was based on whatever was easiest or most convenient. Jim now saw how he cut off action and cut off discussion by his thoughtless response to the distant teammate. He could only imagine how the distant teammate must have felt to have his or her ideas dismissed so easily by the leader.

Arthur said, "Fourth, every knight's ideas are never judged or rejected at the onset. Judgmental words cause defensiveness. Rejection may cause them to drop out or not offer more ideas. Therefore, ideas that don't pass the decision tool test are personally responded to by the king, along with specific information to help the knight strengthen the idea or understand why it was not adopted. The knight must never be led to think or feel the idea was rejected because of friendship or politics."

Jim knew that some of the decisions were made by friendship or politics, not by objective criteria like the decision tool. Jim's team had not yet selected a decision tool although he was committed to helping the team create one the next time they met.

Jim could now see that his responsibility as leader was not to judge the idea. Instead, it was to present to the teammate other issues to consider. He now knew never to say, "That idea will never fly with the directors." Instead, he should make sure he thoroughly understands the idea, and then say, "That idea needs to go before the directors. Let me tell you what some of their concerns are."

Arthur continued, "Fifth, every knight has an equal opportunity to shine. Knights want to show their leadership. Every knight is expected to take a leadership role, and every knight has unlimited opportunities to display their leadership in creating Camelot. The king must actively seek ways to develop and nurture leadership opportunities, including knights the king sees less frequently."

Jim could see he had to develop leadership on the team. Jim had taken the time to select a well-qualified team, but he was reluctant to use the talent that was available because they were distant. He vowed to bring this idea up with the team and to find ways to give everyone more opportunity to bring their leadership to the Tele-Round Table.

The king said, "Sixth, every knight at the Round Table is rewarded or publicly recognized for contributions to Camelot, both at the Round Table and in their individual castles. I have to seek ways the knights would aggressively praise themselves and reward themselves with more opportunities for growth. I had to seek ways the people in the knights' castles could recognize them."

Jim hadn't even considered rewards and recognition. His detailed project plan marked goals and milestones, but Jim never went the extra step to celebrate reaching them. Jim certainly felt a lack of enthusiasm, especially in electronic meetings. Jim always passed off the problem as due to the technology. But the reality was that no one ever praised anyone on the team.

Jim remembered one teammate saying her group worked past midnight to make a critical deadline for the team. Not one person on the team said a word of thanks or recognition. Jim remembered another saying that no one at her location recognized her work, and no one on Jim's worldwide project did, either. It was like living in a no-man's land, she said. Jim now knew he had to do something to help the team generate its own enthusiasm and recognition.

Arthur continued, "Seventh, the king socializes equally with people near and far. If Lance is my honored guest to watch a joust one weekend, other knights must have an equal opportunity on other weekends. Lance should not sit next to me again until every other knight has enjoyed the same honor.

"I also needed to give people at distant castles an equal opportunity to socialize with me. When I visit their castle, I participate in all of the social events that are important to the knight. If I socialize in Camelot with Lance, and then don't socialize at a distant knight's castle with the knight, they will perceive I favor Lancelot more."

Jim had led every meeting from Atlanta. He wondered why he hadn't led some meetings from Europe or Denver. Jim also wondered why he hadn't given each person on the team a chance to lead the meeting from any location. He knew that if Mark led the meeting from an audio link in San Diego that the whole team could become more sensitive to the dynamics of meeting through a variety of technologies.

Jim also decided he needed to talk with Robert about

the problem of envy. He didn't want to end the friendship. But for the project, he had to cool it for a while. Jim decided to raise the issue of his socializing with team members with the team itself. He wanted to become more comfortable with appearing and being more fair in developing social relationships on the team.

When it appeared that Arthur was done with the list, Jim then asked, "How do you create equality when the playing ground is not even, My Liege? In other words, Jim is close and they are far. Are you saying I should keep a list and check off each time I meet with each of my team members?"

Arthur answered. "One day I sat down and made a list. As I went through a week's interaction, it was clear I was spending 50 percent of my time in Camelot and 50 percent outside of Camelot. Distant knights were still complaining to me and Camelot was in collapse. I waited too long. Now that I look back on it, *I should have spent 70 or even 80 percent of my time tending to the needs and relationships of distant knights.* Only then do I think they would have viewed the split as 50-50."

Jim said, "Are you saying you should have spent most of your time traveling, away from Camelot? I just know my budget won't allow me to be away that much time. I am not productive when I am traveling. Besides that, too much business travel hurts my social life here in Atlanta outside of my work. With the hours I work today, I need my social life."

Arthur said, "Jim, I am not suggesting I should have spent 70 percent of my time away from Camelot. Instead,

I should have spent 70 percent of my time *tending to the needs and interests of those that weren't in Camelot.* Part of that effort is visiting each knight on his own turf. The other part is to ensure every knight in every location is fully involved and in the communication leap.

"In other words, I needed to send squires with messages to remote knights. I needed to spend more time getting some of the distant knights to partner with other distant knights on certain pieces of creating Camelot. I needed to send personal notes to distant knights recognizing their accomplishments. I needed to plan better meetings for the limited time we had to meet. I needed to follow up on ideas knights submitted. I needed to make sure that everyone received regular communication from me so they felt important and included. The people in Camelot did not need my time and attention as much as those away from it."

Jim responded, "So, what I hear you saying is that your role was to do whatever was needed to make sure every knight at every castle felt very much a part of building Camelot, even though they were a long distance away from you? You built trust by finding ways that everyone could be involved in a number of ways. You built trust in you as the leader by being extra sensitive to the needs and perceptions of people that were so far away. For success, there has to be no suggestion of favoritism."

Arthur responded, "Yes, Jim. You are correct. Trust is the core, as you know. I had to build trust that everyone felt equally a part of being a Knight at the Round Table.

Favoring one person over another breaks trust. *Even appearances or suggestions of favoritism breaks trust.*"

Jim interjected, "Would it also be fair to say that favoring Robert limits my ability as leader to properly value the input of teammates that are far away? I can think of so many times when I just didn't give any credit to the ideas of people who thought differently than me. Just yesterday, I rejected an idea from Deiter because it was too hard to understand him."

Arthur responded, "I did that, too. I broke the trust of my knights by being too trusting of Lancelot. The knights told me things I didn't want to hear, but I needed to hear. If I had listened, I feel I could have saved Camelot. I know now I could have built a better Camelot because I could have tapped into more ideas than those of just one other person.

"In fact, Jim, I broke the knights' trust in me as their leader every time I failed to act on knowledge they shared with me about Lance or anything else they chose to share. *They trusted me to confront Lancelot on his breach of the code of conduct all Knights of the Round Table swore to obey. It was my role as leader to confront him.*

"I didn't have the courage to do it because he was my friend. Knight after knight asked me to take action on Lancelot's treasonous act. I did not want to listen to those knights. In the void of distance, I didn't have to listen to their complaints. I didn't have to take action. I let myself live in the void, ignoring the problem."

Jim asked, "Are you saying that ignoring the problem

or hiding behind the cover of distance doesn't solve the problem for a remote leader?"

Arthur responded, "You are correct, Jim. Distance restricts what the *knights* will see. Equally as important, it restricts what *you* will see as the leader. That is why it is so critical for kings to listen to all input and to be open to whatever your knights may decide to tell you—even uncomfortable things.

"If the issue is one that conflicts with a basic value of your Tele-Round Table, such as your code of conduct, then it is your responsibility as remote leader to *act* on that information, not to ignore it. *No matter who breaches trust or where they reside, the leader must not hide behind distance and ignore the problem.*

"In my case, Jim, the Knights of the Round Table expected me to take action. My role as king was to build trust and to act in a way that inspired trust. The knights trusted me to act in a way that lived up to the code we all agreed to live by. I made a significant error in judgment by not trusting them enough to listen to their perspective, especially on a core value that set the foundation for trust to flourish."

Jim commented, "When did you know the problem was becoming major?"

Arthur responded, "I saw the distant knights begin to band together in cliques. Individually and collectively, they mocked Lancelot to his face. Eventually, they started to accuse me of weakness behind my back, and later to my face. That is why I reacted as I did when I saw your knights attacking Robert and you. These were important warning signs, Jim.

"My mistake was in how I reacted to the information the Knights of the Round Table shared with me. When some tried to tell me of the negative rumors about Lancelot, I used Excalibur wrongly. I cast it to the throat of the accuser and told him to take his words back or die. Reluctantly, the accuser took back the words."

With intensity in his voice, Arthur continued, "The important point, Jim, is that breakdowns in trust will break down your Tele-Round Table. *Your knights trust you to act consistently and fairly in holding everyone accountable for every factor needed to insure your success.* For me, eventually some of the knights banded together. They are the ones that now hold my castle."

Jim got the message. Jim now knew he relied too much on Robert. He didn't give his distant project members enough meaningful opportunities to shine. He knew he could no longer overlook negative issues, hoping distance would make them go away. Jim committed to take steps to change all three of these.

Jim had one more critical question about trust to ask his mentor.

Merlin

Jim was still struggling with one other level of trust that Arthur had not yet mentioned. That issue was how Jim, as team leader, could comfortably learn to trust people who worked off-site. Because team members were distant, Jim didn't have the opportunities to develop quality relationships as he had with Robert. The thought of trusting anyone outside of Atlanta to do excellent work sent chills up Jim's spine.

Arthur was watching Jim's face while the project leader processed all of the issues on trust. He saw Jim's look of hope and assurance change to one of confusion. Looking at the suddenly pained look on Jim's face prompted Arthur to ask, "The look on your face tells me that you have another question you want to ask me, Jim. Am I right?"

Jim laughed, again surprised by Arthur's perceptiveness. "Yes, Your Majesty. I was thinking about trust. You have helped me get clear about the importance of developing trust. But there is still one issue about trust that I have not yet resolved.

"I have an underlying problem about trust that is rooted in the way I learned to lead. I have a very difficult time trusting my remote knights. I can't observe their work, and the project can't afford for them to make a mistake. I guess I have a very strong need to physically supervise people doing work.

"It is so easy to give work to Robert. I know Robert. I know his work. I trust him implicitly. I do not have anywhere near that level of trust with team members who are distant from me. I don't trust them to do the work competently. I don't know their commitment. Quite frankly, I don't think the people on my project team trust each other, either. The whole business of getting work done across distance makes me uneasy."

Arthur asked, "Tell me more about why you feel uneasy about trusting your distant knights to do competent work out of your view."

Jim could have given a dozen stories where time and resources were wasted doing incorrect work. But he decided to tell Arthur about only one incident.

"I'm uneasy because I've gotten burned a few times, Your Majesty. In order for me to explain the problem, I need to give you some background.

"In the year 2000, there is almost unending pressure for excellence, to the finest detail of products we make and services we deliver. We have to be extremely responsive to our customers. Quality must be next to perfect, and the delivery must be made on time, as promised.

"To be competitive, our project team must meet very rigid quality standards, yet very tight timelines. Missed deadlines can cost us millions of dollars in lost revenues. If any team member fails to meet his or her commitments, our schedule can get thrown back by weeks or months.

"Every problem we have encountered so far on my worldwide team has been from people distant from Atlanta. For example, three weeks ago, I assigned a part of the project to Dieter in Germany. I gave him the directions on what I wanted done, and I gave him two weeks to complete it. I asked him if he understood, and he said he did.

"By the end of the telephone call, I felt we had a clear agreement. I didn't hear from him again until he completed the work. He did his work on time, but it wasn't what I wanted. How do I trust someone who does the work wrong?" pleaded Jim, with a look of exasperation on his face.

Arthur asked, "So, you are upset with Dieter because he did the work wrong?"

Jim said, "Yes! That error caused Phase I to slip about two and a half weeks. My greatest fear is that others will do the same, which I know they will. As it turned out, Robert picked up the pieces and miraculously got us back on schedule again.

"We just don't have time to waste on the project, Your Majesty. We don't have time to fail. Whenever I give work to Robert, I get a good night's rest. Whenever I give it to anyone outside of Atlanta, I don't sleep *at all*. It is really stressful for me to trust anyone off-site to do the work correctly. Did you experience this problem at the Round Table, Your Majesty?"

Arthur responded, "I did not have the same pressure for performance that I sense in your voice. We had pressure of a different sort. Our pressure wasn't to have Camelot built by a specific date, such as September 1. Instead, our pressure was to build Camelot quickly enough to keep the knights motivated to continue working together.

"Remember, Jim, the kings before me set a difficult precedent of plundering and ineffectiveness. Do you remember the story I told you about my first meeting with Sir Sagramore? At first, Sagramore was not only apathetic, but contemptuous that my leadership as king would make a difference. He was not persuaded until I gave him a symbol to believe in, the Round Table.

"Sagramore's attitude was typical of at least half of the knights. The Round Table gave all of the knights a symbol of change and a role in that change. But the Round Table was not enough. The Round Table was a symbol *I* gave to them. It was not one *they created themselves.*

"Therefore, my sense of urgency was to expedite the building of the castle at Camelot. We needed a very quick success that all knights could share in.

"At the Round Table, I engaged the knights' hearts and minds in defining and creating Camelot. But knights want more than talk. Knights are doers. They wanted results, and fast. So we immediately embarked on a tangible landmark the knights would build together—the castle at Camelot. Then Camelot could stand as a symbol they created as a group.

"After talking about Camelot for several days at our first meeting, I remember how eager the knights were to get started building Camelot. Immediately, they were ready to ride their horses back to their castles and begin working on something they would bring back to Camelot six months later. They did not want to wait a minute longer to get started."

Jim could recall the same impatience his team members showed to get started on the project. Jim didn't know if it was the pressure for performance today or something else. But as soon as people got an idea of what they were to do, they wanted to work on it—even though they didn't have all the details.

Arthur continued, "Thank heavens, I was able to persuade the knights to stay one more day. Something in my gut told me I had one more important step to cover with them before they left for their distant castles. Almost reluctantly, they agreed.

"That night, I went to the tree in the forest to meet with Merlin. He was my mentor, and I needed to find out if there was anything else I needed to do before the knights left.

"I was so excited about such an exhilarating day with the knights that my words were tripping all over themselves as they gushed out of my mouth. It was so thrilling to have such a magnificent experience at the Round Table. It was fantastic to see the knights' excitement begin.

"Then Merlin asked, 'Do the knights know what to do while they are at their separate castles for six months?'

"I responded, 'Why, yes, Merlin. They ought to know what to do. We have talked about the castle for two days. Everyone is to bring 50 huge rocks from their castle grounds. We will use these rocks to build the exterior wall and towers. The knights will find the most beautiful rocks, and then transport them to me at Camelot in six months. The knights will be able to build the castle in no time. Then we can mark our first big success as Knights of the Round Table!'"

Jim's mind was tallying up how many tons of rock were to be transported. Moving tons of rock by horse or cart must have been a phenomenally difficult task in Arthur's time. Between the bulk of the rock, the rolling hillside, and the primitive roads, Jim could only imagine the challenge each knight undertook to deliver on his commitment to Arthur.

"Merlin was not smiling. He then said to me, 'What will the castle look like when it is finished, Arthur?'

"I responded, 'It will look like the model I built of Camelot five years ago, Merlin. I told the knights all about the model.'"

Arthur looked at Jim to explain the model. "Jim, the model was blown into the ocean during one bad storm later in the year when I built it. In seconds, a strong gust of wind sucked my days and days of tedious work over the cliff. It was really upsetting to me at the time.

"Merlin's magic powers, though, let me see it again. I didn't see it physically in front of me; rather, I could see it in his crystal ball. Looking at it after all these years, I amazed myself at how beautiful and detailed it was.

"I couldn't resist making a comment about my workmanship to Merlin. 'I did a good job on that castle, Merlin, didn't I? Camelot looks solid and beautiful. I can't wait to see it built in real life, can you?'

"Merlin responded, 'The castle *is* beautiful, Arthur. Did you build a newer model so the knights could see what the completed castle would look like?'

"I told him, 'No, but I described it to them—several times. And everyone talked about special details they wanted to add. They mentioned how exciting the castle would be when it was done.'

"Merlin asked what specifications the knights agreed to for the rocks.

"I responded, 'The knights were to bring big rocks— the most beautiful each knight could find on his land.' "

Once again, Arthur talked to Jim directly. "Merlin had amazingly powerful magic talent, Jim. He could use his crystal ball to look into the future as well as into the past. He motioned me to stand closer to the crystal ball so he could show me the future I created in the meeting today."

Arthur continued, "Merlin asked me, 'Would you like to see what the castle will look like based on the description you have given the knights in your meeting, Arthur?'

"I cheerfully responded, 'Oh, yes! With all of the wonderful ideas the knights shared about the castle, I know that it will be even more beautiful than the model I built five years ago. I can just see it sitting beautifully on top of the hill overlooking the lush countryside.'

"Merlin said, 'I'm going to let you see your next meeting with the Knights of the Round Table six months from now.' I eagerly gazed into the perfectly round ball of glass, hoping the picture I would see there would match or exceed the one in my mind. Such was not the case!

"I was horrified. The castle wasn't at all what I expected. Each knight had brought 50 rocks. But the rocks did not mix well. Some were rough, some were smooth. Some were gray, some were brown. Some were as tall as a man, others were as small as a five-year-old child. Instead of a beautiful castle gracing the top of the hill, there was a huge pile of rocks that looked like they didn't belong together.

"I walked around to the other side of the crystal ball so I could see other parts of the hilltop. I saw Sir Sagramore, Sir Dinadan, Sir Lionel, and eight other knights each try to build different parts of the castle with the rocks each of them brought. Each of them built a separate part of the castle, and none of the parts went together. It was as if the castle was 11 different structures, rather than one. Camelot was a mess!

"I was so upset to see the mess before me. I self-righteously said to Merlin, '*Look at that mess the knights have made! None of them took Camelot seriously. They wasted my time. They lied to me that they cared. They lied to me that they understood my directions. How can I trust knights who can't listen and meet their obligations?*'

"Merlin was taken aback by my words. He asked, 'So, Arthur, you see yourself as betrayed by your knights?' "

Jim was listening intently. The reaction Arthur described was just like his own when Jim's distant team members messed up on the work they promised to do.

Arthur continued, " 'Yes! They betrayed me. Look at them! Not only did they not deliver the rocks correctly, but now they're beginning to fight with one another, just as in the days before I became King. They swore their allegiance, and look how easily they break it!'

"In a flash of time, a number of battles broke out. Some knights made fun of the ideas of the other knights. Others laughed at the gaping holes between the poorly fitted rock towers. Some other knights who brought plain rocks began to disrespectfully deface some beautifully-carved rocks brought by other knights. I even saw one knight, who only brought foot-size stones, teased unmercifully by the others.

"I was totally confused. Pure pandemonium was everywhere in my view. So I asked Merlin, 'I need to understand more about why the knights are fighting.'

"To find the answer, Merlin turned me into a squirrel and sent me into the crystal ball. He gently placed me in the field of rocks and told me to listen to the knights' words as I scurried about the field. It did not take me long to find the answer to my question."

Jim asked, "Why were the knights fighting, Your Majesty?"

"They fought for two main reasons, Jim. First, the knights were bickering with each other about interpretations of the directions I gave at the Round Table six months earlier. I thought every Knight of the Round Table left the first meeting with a clear picture of what they were to do in the time they were apart.

"What I discovered as a squirrel was that the description of Camelot I gave was not clear at all. *Although the miscommunication did not show up for six months, it was obvious that each knight left the room with a completely different interpretation of my words.* Before the knights went off into the distance, I did not insure that everyone had an *absolutely clear picture.*

"I watched in horror as the knights began to draw swords at each other. Some vowed to let God decide who heard my words correctly. They accused each other of being stupid and not really dedicated as a Knight of the Round Table."

Arthur looked directly at Jim and said, "*You* know I didn't want the knights to do battle. Now, just because *I* was unclear, the knights were back to their old habits."

Arthur looked away as he continued, "The second reason the knights were fighting was they were angry about wasting their time and energy. One of the knights spent one whole month finding just the right rocks to bring to Camelot. He could have found 50 rocks just outside the castle. Instead, he was inspired to deliver only the *best* rocks on his land to Camelot. Those rocks the knight selected with such care were now buried among thousands of others. He was upset they sacrificed great amounts of personal time only to find his investment of himself wasted."

Jim felt like someone just hit him in the head with a two-by-four board. Jim wasn't the only one who was frustrated when Deiter came back two weeks later with the wrong work. Now Jim could see how frustrated Deiter must have been wasting two weeks of work time.

Arthur continued his description of his time as a squirrel. He said, "I quickly scrambled by another rock. I heard a conversation between two more knights. One of the two knights brought 50 *huge* boulders to Camelot. He had to use all but three horses in his castle to transport the massive rocks to Camelot. Two of his servants were crushed when one of the boulders rolled off a cart and fell on them. Five of his horses died along the way from the strain. That knight's boulders did little more now than clutter the hillside, as well.

"As I scrambled by other knights, it was clear they all went to great effort and expense to lug the huge rocks all across the country to bring them to me. They were angry beyond description at the mess they faced. Many of the knights were ready to quit."

Jim thought of the time he caused others to waste when directions and agreements were unclear up front. The company lost money, but the people lost resources of their own as well, including their time.

Arthur continued, "Greater than all of their personal frustration, though, the knights were angry with *me*. They trusted *me* to organize the work so Camelot could be built in record time. I broke that trust because I was not clear.

"When Merlin transformed me back into the real world, the experience he put me through had changed my whole focus. Before the experience, I thought the knights broke trust. Now I knew the problem wasn't theirs. *It was mine!* I broke the trust because I wasn't clear."

Jim gulped. Heaven only knew how many times he could have been more clear as the leader. He just never thought about how clarity could build or destroy trust. Now he understood it in very personal terms.

After a short pause, Arthur continued, "Jim, there is no question in my mind that finding ways to be crystal clear in making agreements or giving directions was critical for success, for trust, and for morale. I just learned that talking about something is not enough. I knew I had to find a way to be more clear. If I didn't, I risked losing the Knights of the Round Table, Camelot, and everything the people trusted me to do."

Jim asked, "So, what did you do, Sire?"

Arthur responded, "I was desperate, Jim. I could not afford for the Round Table to fail. The country couldn't afford it, either. So I asked Merlin, 'What can I do to change this picture, Merlin? I thought I was clear with the knights. I thought we had agreement.' "

Jim had said similar words to himself many times before! He remembered making agreements with distant team members, only to get the wrong result back some weeks later.

"Merlin then said, 'Arthur, you said you spent three days talking and describing the castle at Camelot with your Knights of the Round Table. Let's look in the crystal ball at the castle you saw in your mind as you and the knights discussed Camelot.'

"As I peered into the crystal, the castle I saw was identical to the castle I built five years ago. It was the one I had in my head during the Round Table discussion.

"Then Merlin asked, 'I want you now to see into the mind's eye of some of the knights who sat at the Round Table with you. Which knight do you choose?'

"I thought first of one of the knights who sat right next to me, Sir Sagramore. Certainly sitting close to me, his picture would have been similar to mine. When I looked into the crystal, the image Sagramore saw wasn't even close to mine!

"Then I thought about Sir Dinadan. Not only did Dinadan have the image we described today, he also had the benefit of the description we created together in the field years earlier. When I saw the image of Dinadan's mind's eye in the crystal, it, too, was totally different than mine. Dinadan's version of the castle was much taller than mine. It also had fancy towers that could have touched the clouds. It was so complex, even the country's best architects could not have kept it standing, once built.

"I looked into the mind's eye of several more knights. The castles were as different as the knights' faces. None that I saw were even close to my own picture of Camelot.

"The point is, Jim, that each knight framed the image differently. Words or voice alone didn't give me the power to communicate as clearly as I needed to across distance. *Knights who work in isolation have little feedback across distance. So I knew I needed to find a more powerful way to make sure all of the knights shared the same image.*

"Merlin's power to see the future helped me see I

needed to change. It also gave me a chance to decide what to change, so that when the future really arrived, we wouldn't have the disaster I had just viewed in the crystal. Quite naturally, I then asked Merlin, 'What can I do to be more clear?'

"Merlin told me to think of the pile of rocks the knights brought to the hill. Then he said, 'Tell me what you would do differently, Arthur. As you get more clear, I will show you the result in the crystal ball.'

"The person who was, without question, the most clear communicator I had ever known was Merlin. I thought about the things Merlin did that helped me understand him with crystal clarity. I used his three basic techniques to answer.

"I said to him, 'First, I will give them a *visual anchor*—a sharp picture of the castle.'

" 'How? Be specific, Arthur,' said Merlin.

" 'When they are together at the Round Table, I will give them things to *see* so the knights can remember images. I will build a new model, one like the prototype the wind sucked away from me, only this time I'll anchor it down. I'll haul one or more completed rocks into the great hall that houses the Round Table. I'll point out the important features to remember.

" 'Also at the Round Table, I will draw a picture of the castle, or a part of the castle, or the way I want the rock to look, complete with measurements. To help them when they are away in their castles, I will make sure each knight has diagrams to use as a reference during the time he's away from me.'

"Merlin confirmed, 'You are correct, Arthur. One critical way to ensure clarity is to give clear and specific images that show details.'

"After making the first suggestion, I glanced into the crystal ball. I saw some of the rocks on the hill change to be the same size. I also saw some knights organizing the same-size rocks to begin building the castle walls.

"I continued, 'Second is a *hands-on anchor.* I would have a skilled stone cutter show the knights how to cut the stone or carve a design on it. I would even have the knights cut a few stones for practice at the Round Table, *before* they left for their castles. I would have the knights build part of a small model so they could see how the rocks fit together. This activity would ensure the knights will return in six months with the same-size stones, properly cut.'

"Merlin responded, 'You are correct again, Arthur. Another critical way to ensure clarity is to have the knights use their hands or their body. Knights with a hands-on approach to doing work will remember more clearly if they do an activity.'

"After making the second suggestion, the image in Merlin's crystal ball changed again. The irregularly shaped rocks changed to same-size shapes. Now the rocks fit properly together, requiring minimal mud to fill the cracks between the rocks. Now more of the knights were beginning to build some of the castle walls.

"I continued, 'Third is a *word anchor.* Knights need descriptions, definitions, and comparisons. I would make sure we talked in detail about how the structure would look. I would use a lot of analogies or refer to examples elsewhere that were similar. I would pinpoint certain words, dimensions, or concepts that are important. I would open the door for questions.'

"Merlin said to me, 'Right again, Arthur. Get the knights to talk about it. Have discussions that describe Camelot, even the finest details. Encourage discussion and highlight key points or agreements.'

"The image in the crystal ball got even better. The knights were talking with one another and referring to the key points they agreed on earlier. But the image in the crystal ball was still not totally correct.

"Then Merlin continued, 'It is important to highlight key points of an agreement, Arthur. But you must go one more step. You must make sure the distant knight has done more than *hear* you. You must make sure he *understands* you. There is a big difference, you know.' "

Jim interjected, "I should think that after seeing, speaking, and doing they should understand. These three alone go way beyond any clarity I have ever tried with my team. Are you saying these three aren't enough?"

Arthur responded, "Yes, Jim, they're not enough. This last point I will share with you now is one of the most important in really cementing clarity that stays clear after the knights go to their separate castles.

"Knights don't like to be told what to do. They don't like to think they are being talked to as if a child. They don't like to feel like someone else is exercising power over them. So the final step in creating crystal clarity is to create a *clarity partnership* between the knight who is speaking and the knight who is listening. Both of the partner knights must work together to create *understanding*."

Jim questioned, "*A clarity partnership?* How?"

Arthur answered, "Trust was infinitely important to the success of the Knights of the Round Table. When distant, knights can do wrong work for months before others see it or anyone knows it. Misunderstandings about agreements can damage trust significantly.

"To keep trust high, the Knights of the Round Table agreed to create clarity partnerships. Every knight holds the responsibility to build trust by developing a clarity partnership. *We set up an expectation that at the end of every agreement, one person must take the initiative to repeat what he heard, without being asked.*"

Jim interjected, "So you had a system of checks and double-checks that helped insure communication was clear?"

Arthur responded, "Exactly, Jim. And it worked! Clarity let us build trust in each other and trust in the project. That level of trust was critical to our success.

"The most important time for clarity was at the first meeting of the Knights at the Round Table. After all of us dispersed to do our work at a distance, we found ourselves returning to words, diagrams, examples, and discussions at the first meeting. We used all three anchors in the first meeting to be sure we were all in crystal clear agreement. Some knights took the role to clarify and pinpoint critical areas of agreement.

"Over the years that followed, the knights and I referred to those anchors often in the months we were apart.

Those anchors helped us stay focused and build the trust we needed for success."

Jim commented, "My team may be apart from one another for months at a time, too, Your Majesty. We have some pretty fantastic tools to let us communicate while we are distant. Nevertheless, I think my knights need to be just as clear as yours on all critical parts of the project. Communication by E-mail, voice mail, audio conferencing, and other technologies just isn't as clear as when we talk face to face in one location.

"What communication did you maintain while the knights worked from their castles?"

Arthur responded, "In order to keep momentum flowing during the time the knights were separated, we used a variety of ways to keep the knights in touch with each other and with us.

"We sent squires and ambassadors to remote castles. And I traveled about three months out of the year myself. It was very important for me to make the effort to meet each knight on his own turf. It gave me a chance to foster a more personal relationship with each knight without the interference of all of the other knights.

"We also used a lot of birds."

Jim asked, "Birds?"

Arthur responded, "It was important to keep communication flowing when knights were at their castles. Otherwise, they'll forget about you across distance."

Jim interjected, "Do you mean *out of sight, out of mind?*" Jim had heard people on his worldwide team use these words many times.

Arthur responded, "Yes, Jim. When knights were out of sight, we kept them in mind by creating a specific communication plan. We decided what we were to communicate, when, and how.

"Sometimes information was very important and we needed a response. Other times, the information was less important. All of the time, though, we needed to keep the communication flowing between my location and theirs, so Camelot was in their conscious awareness.

"We had three kinds of birds that we used to send messages back and forth. White pigeons meant the message was urgent, and the knight was expected to respond as soon as the pigeon landed. Gray and white spotted pigeons meant the message was routine. The knight was expected to respond by the same time the next day. Solid gray pigeons meant the message was for information only. It required no response."

Jim made the connection to his voice mail and E-mail systems. Both had a priority system that no one ever used. Jim liked Arthur's priority system, and he liked the fact that the knights agreed on response times. Slow response on E-mail and voice mail was a constant complaint of just about everyone on his worldwide team.

Jim said, "No group I have ever worked for had talked about how we would communicate, or when, or by which means. It appears that you had a very specific plan that bridged the distance when you and your knights were apart."

Arthur responded, "That's right, Jim. We knew we couldn't see each other for months. Yet, we had to keep everyone informed of the most critical information. If some knight got left out, he'd be upset. So we did have a plan for how we would communicate across distance.

"For example, every Monday I sent out important news for the week. It was a real sight to see 60 pigeons all fly out of Camelot at the same time to take messages to the knights. The pigeons let me reach out to the knights I couldn't see. It was one of many ways I kept contact alive and progress moving forward.

"There is one more point that is important for you to know, Jim. At first, when the knights tried to communicate by birds, the messages were too long. Pigeons are only strong enough to carry short messages. If the knights sent messages that were too long, the pigeons couldn't fly above the trees. We lost a lot of birds that way.

"So we had to create a format that allowed us to be brief, yet clearly indicate if a response or action was needed."

Jim remembered being frustrated just this morning reading a five-page E-mail message that gave no clue what Jim was to do with it. He had no idea why one of his team members sent it to him. He didn't know what action to take on it.

Arthur helped Jim see that he needed to establish a concise format for E-mail, voice mail, and other store-and-forward communication on his team. *Jim made a mental note to have his team agree on some formats and response times to include in the communication plan.*

Arthur added, "*They also had to learn when to send a message by pigeon, when by ambassador, and when to wait for a personal visit. Most routine information was sent by pigeon.*

"There was one kind of communication, though, we never sent by pigeon—negative communication. Negative communication sent by pigeon caused a lot of friction between the knights. The knights agreed never to send negative news by pigeon or any other messenger. Negative interaction was always done face to face, so the knights could talk back and forth."

Jim remembered a scathing E-mail message he had received two days earlier. The person who sent it didn't have the facts, and made numerous negative conclusions. The person also copied it to Jim's boss. Jim was so angry about the message, he had to leave work early to calm down. How much better it would have been to have talked face to face, one-on-one video conference, or even *tactfully* by phone, about the issue.

Jim responded, "That sounds like a foundation even my knights today could use, Your Majesty. Let me take the responsibility to ensure clarity for what you have shared with me today, My Liege. There are four steps to creating the level of clarity that is needed when people work at a distance. First is to let people see it. Second is to let them talk about it. Third is to let them do it. And lastly is to have the other partner reflect it."

Arthur said, "You have it, Jim! You have the secret recipe for creating the level of clarity your knights need when they work across distance."

Jim responded, "I will propose to the team that we use Merlin's strategy to clarify each agreement, Your

Majesty. I feel it will help us substantially in being more clear in the agreements we make."

"I am glad you found it useful, Jim. It is a powerful way to build trust at your worldwide Tele-Round Table."

As Jim exited the meeting with Arthur, he reflected on all of the times trust had been broken because of miscommunication. In every case, the team members tried to do right work. Miscommunication made them do it wrong. Jim was suddenly embarrassed about all the times he accused others of a breach of trust or a lack of caring when the problem was something he did himself. He needed to be more clear.

Then Jim remembered what his mom always used to tell him. "When you point your finger at someone else, just remember three fingers are pointing back at you!" He decided to call her to say thanks for the great advice.

The Fall

hen Jim and Arthur connected Saturday morning, Jim was concerned. Instead of Arthur's jovial, happy manner, the king's demeanor was somber. Something significant had changed during the night. Jim feared that the moment of Arthur's battle for Camelot was at hand. The knights on the field near Arthur had become more active in recent days. Arthur had less time to talk as he was constantly interrupted by knights with messages.

When they first connected with one another, both stood silently for a period of time that could not be measured in minutes and seconds. Without saying a word, both men felt a sadness suddenly descend upon them that made their bodies and spirits heavy.

Arthur was sitting in a field. His elbows were resting

on his knees. His eyes were cast toward the ground that would soon capture his blood and surround his dead body.

Finally, Arthur spoke. "I am afraid the battle for Camelot is at hand, Jim. My lead knights tell me we are less than two days from our war against the enemy knights who took away Camelot. I may be only two days from my mortality! There is no way I can express to you how I feel, with my life on this earth now measured in such a brief, finite time. I have so much to do, Jim. Yet I am almost out of time."

Jim could see Arthur's eyes water. Jim didn't know what to say to Arthur. He didn't want *any* battle to occur that would take away his friend and mentor.

Among the thousands of thoughts that flashed through his mind, Jim wished he could step through the mirror to help Arthur. He wished he could send some powerful technology from the year 2000 to save Arthur's kingdom. But he couldn't. Both men were trapped in their own centuries, never to shake each other's hands or pat each other on the back.

A chill shivered its way up Jim's spine as an ominous feeling overcame him. Desperately, Jim asked, "What can I do for you, My Liege? You have been so much a part of my life for the last few weeks that I shudder to think our time to talk will soon end.

"How do I thank you for the richness you have brought to my life? You have given me precious knowledge that I promise you I will use. You have shared stories of your life that I will take with me daily. The friendship we have created across time will be with me the rest of my life. I want to help you, Sire, but don't know how."

Arthur, too, spoke with emotion. "All that you have said of me, Jim, I say back to you. The preview of the year 2000 is *spectacular*! It makes me happy to see how free and creative people are in your world. It has been fun to mentor you, as Merlin did me, to lead effectively across distance.

"Although I live in the first millennium and you are about to enter the third, it is amazing how much we have in common as leaders. That must be because leadership is a people process. It has been exciting to help you create your own Tele-Round Table, Jim. In this bleak time, you have brought joy to my dark world."

Arthur had to pause for a moment to regain his composure and restore calmness to his face that quivered with anxiety. Jim listened eagerly for his mentor's words.

Arthur finally spoke, "Like a battle axe crashing into my chest, I find my legacy crashing against me again, Jim. I feel haunted again by the urgency to leave my mark on the world. I just *can't* be forgotten in history! I am a *king*! I am *real*. I led the creation of Camelot—a place the *world* should know and enjoy!

"I need to leave a *positive* legacy that is undisputed in your history books, Jim. I need to do something concrete that makes your world better. I want to leave a legacy that is alive and wonderful in your time.

"Right now, the only thing I know I will leave is a void. I leave only the void of which you spoke when we first met—being lost to history."

The words tugged at Jim's heart. Jim could relate to Arthur's need to make a noble mark that would stand the test of time. Perhaps it is a need of those whose quest it is to be a great and effective leader.

With emotion and confidence in his voice, Jim spoke, "You have *not* left a void, Your Majesty. In fact, few leaders in history have distinguished themselves as you have done through the legend that survives you."

Jim had a surprise he had been working on for several weeks to present to Arthur. Ever since their first conversation, he knew Arthur wanted to preserve his place in history. Despite the king's own needs, Arthur spent the last several weeks mentoring Jim without asking anything for himself.

Jim knew that now the time had arrived to act on his surprise. His royal friend was needing a tele-friend across time who could assure the royal majesty of his life in Jim's world.

Arthur was surprised to see a smile suddenly break through the melancholy look on Jim's face. Jim spoke, "I have a surprise to show you today, Your Majesty. I want to show you some of the life of your legacy that will survive long beyond my own life."

In a flash, Jim grabbed his small hand mirror and drove to the local library. He could hardly drive there fast enough to show Arthur his first surprise.

Arthur had only seen a handful of books in his entire life. Now through the eye of a mirror, Arthur saw a wonderful place called a library. Arthur was awestruck at the thousands of books that lined the shelves.

Jim walked directly to the children's section where the featured books for the week were about King Arthur and Camelot. In the children's section, about 20 children were gathered around an adult reader who was dressed like a knight. The children, aged from 4 to 10 years, were enthralled by the story of the Knights of the Round Table.

Jim turned the mirror so Arthur could see the looks on the children's faces. Little boys and little girls were totally engulfed by the story. Each lived the legend in his or her mind, as the reader told the tale of King Arthur, Gwynevere, and Lancelot.

After the story, the children asked many questions of the reader-knight. The children wanted to know more about Arthur. So the knightly reader walked the children over to the books on the topic. Stories of Camelot lined an entire shelf! In a flash, every child had at least one book about King Arthur and the Knights of the Round Table in his or her hands to take home and read! And enjoy! And learn about life!

Jim walked over by the computers. He keyed in KING ARTHUR, and screens of listings showed Arthur all of the articles and references written about him. Jim probed at a deeper level, bringing the text of some of those articles to the screen. Arthur loved the resources the computer brought with the touch of a few keys.

Jim then walked to the fiction section of the library. He showed Arthur the stacks of books about him and his time. Arthur could hardly believe all of the books written about him. He suddenly realized that although nothing tangible survived *from* his time, much tangible survived *about* his time. It made his heart feel better.

Jim grabbed a few of the books, checked them out, and then left the library. He vowed to read some of the stories to Arthur later.

When Jim got back into his car, he saw Arthur in the rearview mirror. Arthur no longer had the melancholy look. Instead, a smile covered his face from ear to ear. Arthur asked many questions about books and libraries and computers.

Arthur was much happier about his legacy. But Jim wasn't done yet.

"I have another surprise, Sire. All day today, The Movie Channel is having a Camelot-a-thon!"

Arthur asked, "A Camelot-a-thon? What is that?"

Jim tried to explain it as best he could. "A Camelot-a-thon is 12 hours straight of movies on a certain theme. The theme today is—guess what—King Arthur and Camelot! At 1:00, we'll watch *Excalibur*. Then we'll watch the movie *Camelot*, which is a musical. If you want to see still others, we'll drive to the video store to select some others that will interest you, as well. *Excalibur* and *Camelot*, though, are my two favorites about you, Your Majesty."

Jim got home and tried to indoctrinate Arthur to the concept of a couch-potato. He knew that four hours of movies would be a strain on a man who was used to the physical activity of a king.

Arthur surprised Jim by asking, "What is a potato, Jim?"

Jim didn't realize that England had no potatoes in Arthur's time. So Jim had to dig one out of the refrigerator. A bachelor now, Jim didn't keep up with throwing away old fruits and vegetables in the fridge. All he could find was an old potato that had some white roots growing out of it. So, Jim grabbed it anyway, and showed Arthur what it looked like. Arthur laughed at how funny it looked.

Jim also showed Arthur popcorn. Jim popped a bag in the microwave, and then showed Arthur the fluffy white puffs. "Popcorn and movies go together, Your Majesty. It is customary in the year 2000 to get some food you like to snack on during a movie, because we're going to be here for a while."

Jim suggested Arthur get some snacks to eat because the movies would take a while. Arthur did.

Arthur *loved* the movie *Excalibur*. He told Jim that the historical context shown in the movie was fairly accurate. Arthur said the only incorrect part was the actor who played Arthur's part in the movie.

"At 20, I was more handsome than the movie star that played me," Arthur said. Jim had heard that comment by every male who was portrayed in a movie by a Hollywood actor. In fact, the only time a male liked the star was when Tom Cruise played the part!

Arthur was sitting at the edge of his seat during most of the movie *Excalibur*. He was in awe of the vividness of the action and the realism of the scenery. He felt the story line was quite accurate and reflected the mood of the year

597. "In the movie, you can really see the emotion of how tough it was to be a knight in my time."

At Jim's coaching about movie ratings, Arthur rated the movie *Excalibur* at 4 out of 4 possible stars.

Jim decided to lighten the king's mood, so he said, "You want to leave a historical legacy, My Liege. Let me share one with you. You are Arthur, King of England, *creator* of Camelot, *leader* of the Round Table, and *movie critic* extraordinaire!"

Arthur laughed. Jim had helped Arthur escape the pain of the royal majesty's real world—if even for a few moments. Arthur was thirsty to find out as much as he could about his legacy in the very limited time he had left.

Then the next movie began—*Camelot*—with Richard Harris and Vanessa Redgrave. Arthur was thoroughly engrossed in the movie and the songs. As Jim gazed in the mirror during the movie, Jim caught Arthur smiling and laughing. The king was captivated by the movie.

At the end of the story, the movie's Arthur met a small boy on the field outside the castle at Camelot. Through the mirror, Jim saw the real Arthur's face show a smile and tears at the same time. Spontaneously, Arthur said, "That really happened, Jim! I saw the boy yesterday!"

During the ending credits of the movie *Camelot*, Arthur said, "How beautifully that movie captured the essence of Camelot, Jim! Do you remember when I told you that Camelot was not just an empty castle. Instead it was a way of life that everyone cared deeply about. That movie captured what it was like. Camelot *does* live in your time! It lives through the books and the movies and the legend."

Arthur felt happier in his heart than he had felt earlier in the day. But he was still compelled to clarify his place in history. Since Jim lived in the future, Arthur asked, "How many other great monarchs in England are as well known as I in the year 2000, Jim?"

Jim was a history buff, so Arthur's question was easy to answer. "Several kings and queens of England are well known in my time, My Liege. Of those in history, perhaps the best known from England is Henry VIII. He is in all the history books.

"Many know King Henry VIII had eight wives, some of whom lost their heads over him, literally."

Arthur asked, "What might a person find about him in the library or the video store, Jim?"

Jim was happy to respond, "Books and movies have been written about his life, too, Your Majesty. But Henry VIII is not painted as a kind and caring king as you are. Instead, he is more like the kings that preceded you. I would have to say he learned no lessons from you about valuing people, My Liege."

Prompted by more questions from Arthur, Jim described more of the other historical royalty of England. Jim included those he saw entombed at Westminster Abbey several weeks earlier. He even talked briefly about Prince Charles and Diana, including the dilemma of who would serve as the next monarch of England—Charles or his son.

In Arthur's world, a knight suddenly interrupted him.

As soon as the knight left, Arthur looked again at Jim with a somber expression.

With words weighted and flattened with sadness, Arthur said, "The battle is to begin at sunrise." Arthur bit his lower lip, knowing his time was even shorter than he expected. His mind was whirling to make the final decision about how he wanted to preserve his rightful place in history as a great monarch of England. Less than a half day was left until Arthur's battle and probable death.

Arthur suddenly spoke, "Jim, I have thought about my legacy for several weeks. After my day with you today, I finally have the answer to my dilemma. I know what I need to do to cement my legacy.

"When we first met, Jim, we agreed to help one another. You have helped me immensely today. But I have one more favor to ask."

Jim was eager to support Arthur. "*Yes*, Your Majesty. Just tell me what you want, and I will do it."

Despite the painful reality of his imminent death, Arthur's face showed a calmness and peace greater than Jim had seen since they had met.

Arthur spoke, "The legend that has survived me is beautiful, Jim. I cannot tell you how wonderful it is to have stepped into your world to see the legacy that lives about Camelot.

"When you and I first met, I felt that legacy alone was like not existing at all. Now that you have helped me see the depth of that legacy, I know that I will die a happy and fulfilled man.

"A part of me, though, wants to leave something tangible that *proves* I existed and that sets the date of Camelot's fall." With those words, Arthur pulled two scrolls from a pack on his horse. He rolled them open, one at a time, so Jim could see the contents.

Arthur said, "I have two maps to show you, Jim. These maps will help you find the location of the castle where I was raised."

Arthur held up the first map so Jim could see it. The map showed all of England. "You must draw a copy of this map as best you can. I do not know if this castle survives to your time. So this map will help you find the coastline where the castle exists now in my time."

Jim carefully sketched the map. He drew an arrow pointing to the general location Arthur identified where he grew up. When Jim signaled he had the map drawn, Arthur pulled out the second scroll to show the second map. The second map was a very detailed picture of the coastline by the castle. To Jim, it looked like a close-up view of part of the first map.

Arthur spoke, "This second map gives you a very close view of the cliffs near the castle where I was born. The castle sat high on a cliff overlooking the ocean. The cliff near the castle had a very distinctive shape. It is *very important* that you carefully detail the unique shape of the cliff, *exactly* as you see it here.

"I want you to go to this exact location where I will leave something for you. I do not want to tell you what I will leave. Instead, I will only tell you where to go so you can find it. You must find this field and go to this exact location I have marked with an X."

Jim was very careful to draw every line in proportion to every other line of the coast. They checked the preciseness of the duplicate drawing and revised a few lines as Arthur specified, until Arthur was comfortable that Jim had a map that would stand the test of time.

When the map was done, Arthur pointed to a location on the map and said, "As a child, I used to play in a cave near the top of the cliff. In my day, no one knew it was there but Merlin and me. The cliff is so steep, though, a person cannot climb down to it unassisted. You'll have to climb down on a rope."

Jim could hardly wait to find the cave. He marked every detail so his map was sure to be accurate. He used every principle to be crystal clear in understanding Arthur's directions. He used every technique Arthur taught him, including the clarity partnership. Jim knew he would not have a chance to return to Arthur for more information later—or ever!

Jim asked, "How far down do I climb?"

Arthur responded, "About the height of three men standing on top of one another. In my time, I attached a rope to the trees that grew close to the cliff. I will leave something for you in the cave that will *prove* I existed."

Jim was ready to leave right then and there. He said excitedly, "I promise I will go there tomorrow, Your Majesty. I will take vacation, buy my ticket, and be there in only hours."

The look on Arthur's face became serious again. Jim knew from the king's expression to pay attention.

Arthur exclaimed, "*No!* Don't go yet, Jim. I want you

to wait until you have been able to do everything I have detailed for you to do with your Tele-Round Table.

"You must promise me you will not go to the cave until you have created a legendary team that circles the world. Only after you know you have achieved high level trust with everyone on your worldwide project and achieve a top worldwide result should you make the trip. Do you promise me you will do that, Jim?"

Whatever the king asked, Jim knew he would do. It was easy to reassure Arthur. "I promise, My Liege. I will create the trust you have helped me know is so critical. Only then will I seek your gift of proof that you will leave in the cave."

Arthur sat back and breathed a sigh of relief. He trusted Jim to do exactly what he agreed to do. At the same time, Arthur knew his time to bid farewell to Jim was at hand.

The king spoke. "You have taken me on an incredible journey, Jim. Now I must take care of planning yours. I must make the trip to the cave to leave the gift for you and the world.

"I know you will be successful, Jim. I trust you will work to achieve the level of trust you seek. As I say good-bye to you my heart is full of joy that we have had this wonderful opportunity to meet across the ages."

Jim responded, "Thank you also, My Liege, for an equally incredible journey. You have helped me understand how to really engage people in working as partners together, though split by distance. I will take every experience we have shared across the millennia."

With a lump in his throat and a tear in his eye, Arthur said, "Good-bye my friend, Jim. Godspeed!"

Jim was so full of emotion he could hardly speak above a whisper. "Good-bye, Your Majesty. May God be with you as well!"

Sadly, he watched Arthur jump on his horse and ride away into the distance.

The Gift

A t the end of the month, Jim brought his world-wide project team together for a four-day meeting. It was the best investment his company ever made. The *Knights of the Tele-Round Table* left that meeting with a foundation of trust that allowed real teamwork across distance to happen.

Over the next months, Jim used every strategy Arthur taught him. Jim was surprised to see the people on the team notice the changes. They not only gave Jim their approval of the new strategies, but they began to model them, as well. Using the symbols of Camelot, Excalibur, the Round Table, the Joust, Lancelot, and Merlin, Jim targeted critical factors that made a difference.

Within nine months, the team experienced a complete turnaround. They built communication bridges that bridged the geographic distance and the interpersonal distance that had divided them before. At last, they were truly global.

At the end of the first year, the team exceeded its production goal by 30 percent. Customer service ratings were at a record high. The team received the company's prestigious quality award and were honored personally by the company's president. The worldwide team was featured in *Fortune Magazine* as a model for other virtual teams in the organization. Tom Peters even included a profile of them in his latest best-selling book.

Jim now felt he had achieved the success of which Arthur spoke. Arthur had given Jim the gift of how to lead across distance. Now Jim was to give Arthur his gift.

Jim pulled out the maps to find the cave that Arthur played in as a child. He took the copies of his hand-drawn maps to the library. It was a long, arduous task, but he finally found a match. A small English village existed in the spot Arthur had marked with the X. Jim could hardly wait to find the cave that awaited him there.

Jim bought his ticket and was on his way to London the following day.

* * *

After landing at Heathrow, Jim made his way to Victoria Station. He bought a first-class train ticket and settled in for his several-hour journey to the village. Jim took a taxi to a comfortable bed-and-breakfast inn. He immediately began his foot journey to find the cliff that Arthur had pinpointed on the map.

Jim spent the rest of the day trying to find the cliff. Before he was ready to end his search, darkness had arrived. After so many months of anticipation, Jim was suddenly filled with disappointment. He reluctantly found his way back to the inn. His mood was so deflated he could hardly eat dinner, and barely got to sleep. This task was going to be more difficult than he imagined.

In the morning at breakfast, Jim tried to get the server's attention. He motioned for her to come to his table. Armed with a coffee pot that she knew the American visitor wanted, she sported the name tag Morgana. Arthur asked Morgana if she recognized the point on the map that Jim had marked. She said no, she didn't.

Disappointed, Jim asked the front-desk attendant if she knew where the point was. The attendant did. She suggested he rent a bicycle and travel north along a dirt road. She estimated the cliff was eight kilometers or so away. Jim went back to his room to don his backpack, water bottles, and rope, and left.

Jim rented the bicycle and began his trek up the road. About 20 minutes later, he thought he had found the point. The coastline made the unique turn that Arthur pointed out on the map. Jim knew he hadn't gone eight kilometers. He was so convinced he was in the right place, though, that he decided to take a closer look before biking further north.

Jim could hardly bike across the field fast enough. Because the ground was a little mushy, Jim had to stop riding the bicycle and began to walk it. His body pumping with adrenaline, Jim decided to abandon the bike and run toward the cliff.

As he got nearer to the cliff, however, he suddenly realized he was not alone. In the distance was a person, a woman walking slowly across the field. As Jim got closer, he thought he recognized the outfit the woman was wearing. But he couldn't place where he had seen it.

As he got closer to her, Jim decided to call to her. Not knowing who it was, he just yelled in a friendly American way, "Hey, there! Do I know you?"

As soon as she heard his words, the woman stopped her trek across the field and turned her head toward Jim. She returned Jim's wave, and flashed a smile that somehow Jim did not trust.

All of a sudden, Jim knew who the woman was. It was Morgana, the server at the inn. What was she doing here? She said she didn't know where this place was.

The last words Jim remembered hearing Morgana say were, "This is a great place to pick berries." By the time Jim realized Morgana was a sorceress from Arthur's time, she had cast a magic spell on Jim that sent him into a deep sleep.

Because Morgana was a sorceress, she was not constrained by time like Arthur was. As soon as Jim fell to the ground, she pulled the backpack off his back. She yanked the hand-drawn maps from the main compartment of the pack. She frantically tied Jim's hands with the rope, and then headed to the point that Jim had marked on the map.

She made her way over to the cliff. She began an intense search in the bushes and thickly forested trees that bordered near the cliff. In only minutes, she had left Jim and the rest of the world behind as she searched for Arthur's gift. She wanted it. Her only revenge was to keep Arthur out of recorded history. Now was her chance to do just that.

After Morgana was out of view, another man appeared by Jim. The long fingers of the man's left hand brushed an arc in the air just above Jim's sleeping body. As soon as the man completed his hand arc, suddenly Jim began to awaken from the deep sleep of Morgana's spell.

When Jim opened his eyes, the old man's eyes were peering into his. Jim did not recognize the old man, yet he felt he knew him somehow.

With the swiftness of an eagle, the man untied Jim's hands. Softly, he said, "Arthur sent me."

A chill went up Jim's spine. He didn't know what was happening, but he felt he was not dreaming now. Who had Arthur sent? Who was this man?

The man said firmly, "Come with me *now*. We have no time to waste. Morgana will sense I am here soon."

The man grabbed Jim's backpack and began to run north across the field. As Jim tried to track the man, his sleepy body felt like it was made of lead weights. Jim jogged as fast as he could, but he couldn't have been doing even a third of normal running speed.

As he tried to keep up with the other jogger, Jim wondered how the man next to him knew the name of the woman. After running for less than two minutes, Jim was breathing so hard he had to stop. The spell Morgana cast on him drained him of his energy. With too little oxygen in his lungs to speak, Jim's eyes implored the stranger to speak.

Before Jim could speak the question, the man responded, "I am Merlin. Arthur sent me to meet you here. Arthur knew Morgana would try to find the gift. So he marked the wrong place on the map to divert her. He marked a place close enough that you and I could find one another. But he marked it far enough away that she could not capture the gift for herself."

Jim smiled! Then he felt a sudden burst of energy. It was as if he broke through a shell that drained him, and now he was free. "Let's go, Merlin. Quickly!"

They continued to race across the field. As they neared the forest near the cliff, they quickly tied the rope around the base of a gnarly old tree. Merlin threw the loose end of the rope over the cliff and motioned for Jim to climb down it.

Jim no longer knew if he was awake or asleep, but he decided to go with the flow. He grabbed onto the rope and cascaded over the side of the cliff. After descending about 20 feet, there he stood at the opening of a large cave.

Jim made the mistake of looking back toward the Atlantic Ocean which sent its roaring waves crashing on the rocks about 150 feet below. The steep grade gave Jim a sense of urgency to get his feet on solid ground inside the cave. Jim anchored his feet at the cave opening and peered inside. The cave was masked in total darkness within three feet from the opening.

"How am I ever going to find the gift in this darkness?" Jim said, frustrated that he had not brought a match or a flashlight. About that moment in time, though, Jim thought he saw a bright shimmer deeper into the cave. The shimmer beckoned Jim to come closer. So he carefully felt that his feet were on a solid surface before he slowly and carefully transferred his weight with each new step.

After taking several steps in pitch darkness, finally Jim's left toe hit a hard surface. Jim thought the lump in front of his toe was a rock. As soon as his foot touched it, the sun shone brightly into the cave. The entire room lit up as bright as day.

In front of Jim, embedded in the rock, was Excalibur! Jim's mouth dropped open, as he whispered its name in wonder, "*Excalibur!*" *Arthur* had held that sword 1400 years ago. Jim knew that when he touched the sword now, that would be the closest to a handshake he could ever have with his royal friend.

Jim remembered the excitement when Arthur first told him about how only a great leader could pull the sword free of the rock. Was the sword anchored again? Could only a great king remove it?

Before Jim could reach out and touch Excalibur, his eyes looked at the walls of the cave. Arthur had written with colored rock all over the walls. He drew a picture of the castle at Camelot. He drew a map with the location of where Camelot stood. He wrote the names of Sir Lancelot, Merlin, and all of the wonderful parts of the legend that now Jim knew well. He signed his name and wrote the year 597.

And then Jim saw another message. The message was

to Jim. Arthur wrote *Jim's* name. "To my friend, Jim Smith, Knight of the Tele-Round Table!"

"Thank you Arthur, my friend and king!" said Jim as he reached to touch Excalibur.

Suddenly Jim realized why Arthur told him to wait until his worldwide team had become an extraordinary team. Had Jim become a great enough leader to free Excalibur from the rock?

Jim put his left hand on the left arm of the hilt. Maybe it was Jim's imagination, but did he feel it move? Jim put his right hand on the right arm of the hilt. Was any of this real?

Jim's heart was beating at an all-time high rate, fueled by the adrenaline of knowledge that Arthur had placed the sword there.

Jim anchored his feet squarely in front of the sword. And then, with all his might, he pulled. . . .

Arthur's Insights

When trust flourishes, people do magical,
wonderful things together—
like create Camelot.

Excalibur

As remote leader, when your team is distant from you, you have little or no power and control over them. In the isolation of distance, the only power and control you have as remote leader is what your remote team members exercise over themselves.

The key way to build high performance across distance (to give you and your team power and control over the result) is to build trust. Be obvious that every word, every action, every initiative on the virtual team builds trust . . .

- In you as virtual[1] leader.

---

[1]Virtual means multi-site. Virtual comes from the concept of virtual reality. Any group that is not co-located is virtual.

- In the virtual project or virtual organization.
- In all virtual partners across distance.

The Round Table

Since virtual projects don't share a common work space, a virtual team needs strong symbols to unite people across distance.

- Bring people together for a project launch meeting.
- Make sure each partner values the benefit each reaps directly (and personally) by being a member of the virtual partnership.
- In the void of distance, structure a way the team can amplify its accomplishments while distributed. Be creative, yet personal, in giving each other frequent recognition of all that the virtual team accomplishes together.

The Joust

Since virtual partners have limited interaction and limited knowledge of each other in their isolation, the virtual team must establish many ways to help the partners learn about each other quickly and frequently.

- Establish ways for the team to learn more about each other professionally and personally (one-site meetings, electronic yearbooks, site previews) so they will collaborate even when distant.
- Establish a short, informal compressed meeting for the team to talk with one another, to problem-shoot and

have others contribute (e.g., the Friday Joust audiocon-ference).

- Since virtual partnering doesn't come naturally, struc-ture pairs of people to work together on parts of the project. Better yet, encourage them to do so.
- Be an idea champion. Value every idea presented at your Tele-Round Table. Handle it in a way that seems fair to the person who offered it.
- Since trust is fragile, especially at first, react on an as-sumption of trust, not distrust.

Camelot

People who work across distance tend to lose focus after any single-site meetings. Therefore, it is critical that the virtual team create:

- A clear, compelling intellectual link so every virtual part-ner knows exactly where the team is headed once every-one is distributed.
- A clear emotional link on a very personal level so each remote partner stays motivated when distant.
- A daily decision tool that is used as each person does work remotely to align work and effort worldwide.

Lancelot

Be *scrupulously fair* in treating all team members, near and far, equally. Even appearances or suggestions of favoritism break trust.

- Avoid the temptation to rely more on those on-site with you than those at a distance.
- Balance the needs of the knights near and far.
- Give every tele-knight an equal opportunity to excel and contribute to the result.
- Confront nonperformance. Don't let problems and poor performance fade or be ignored in distance.
- Be consistent and fair in holding everyone accountable for every factor needed to insure your success.

Merlin

Miscommunication, inequities of information, and unequal access to information are significant trust-breakers on remote teams. The impact of these remote problems may not show up for months, but will always negatively impact productivity and profits across distance.

Therefore, to be extremely clear when making all agreements, secure crystal clarity by using these anchors:

- *Visual anchors*—pictures, graphs, charts, images
- *Hands-on anchors*—feel, touch, manipulate it
- *Verbal anchors*—words and details, analyses, comparisons, steps, processes.

Anchor clarity with a clarity partnership, where one person repeats what was heard, without being asked. The clarity partnership helps people split by distance to share critical context and details that typically are missing when people work in isolation. Later, if the distant group members can't reach one another spontaneously, each has sufficient information from which to make an effective independent decision.

Keep communication flowing to counteract the out of sight, out of mind phenomenon on distributed teams. Create a communication plan to make sure everyone is informed about basic team issues.

The Excalibur Award

*To promote, develop, and
recognize effective leadership
of distributed work groups*

To be competitive in the world marketplace, today's leaders will be faced with an increasing need to create effective distributed work groups. Today's leaders need new tools and techniques to achieve top performance with people who work from different locations, different companies, and different countries. They also need new strategies to create inspired people who stay motivated and focused in the isolation of distance.

This book's message begins to open a key door to effective work groups: building trust. Whether you are trying to bridge the interpersonal distance or the geographic distance that separate people, the success factors Arthur related in this book are critical to your success.

If you are looking for additional, more specific tools and techniques to improve your *distributed* work group, you may be interested in three of our training programs that are uniquely tailored with tools and techniques that managers, leaders, and distributed team members can use to improve performance across distance. Three key training programs include:

- **Leading a Remote Work Group:** Learn from the best practices of leaders of successful distributed work groups, large or small. This *unique* research-based workshop covers a five-part model that will help you understand what you must do differently as a remote leader.

- **Teamwork Without Walls:** *Techniques to Create Unity and Performance Across Distance.* Learn from the best practices of successful *distributed* work groups. This unique research-based workshop and team intervention covers a four-part model that will help the remote team create a foundation for high performance, despite distance.

- **Electronic Communication:** *Techniques to Communicate Effectively and Humanly in Compressed Mode.* This cutting-edge workshop helps people who communicate mostly through technologies (videoconference, audioconference, voice mail, E-mail, and other groupware) to be more effective.

After the training programs, the remote leader or remote team can qualify for the Excalibur Award. The Excalibur Award program is designed to give remote leaders and remote teams an incentive to use the tools and techniques presented in the workshops. Once the remote leader or remote team shows proof it has applied the model presented in the workshop, the leader or team will receive the Excalibur Award.

For more information about the Excalibur Award program and the remote leadership, remote teamwork, and remote communication training programs, please contact:

Bridge the Distance, International
8378 East Jamison Circle South
Englewood, CO 80112-2756 U.S.A.

Within the U.S.A., call
1-800-694-9099

Outside the U.S.A., call
(303) 694-9099 Office
(303) 694-9091 Facsimile

About Jaclyn Kostner, Ph.D.
The Distance Doctor

JACLYN KOSTNER, Ph.D., is president and founder of Bridge the Distance, International, a consulting and training firm headquartered in Englewood, Colorado. The firm's niche market specializes in high performance *virtual (geographically split) work groups,* including:

- Alliances with customers, suppliers, and other vendors
- Downsized staffs that must share resources across distance
- Sales or service organizations that span multiple locations
- Cross functional teams where team members don't report to the leader
- Remote manufacturing, internationally shared R & D, or other remote groups
- Strategic partnerships and other virtual organizations
- Telecommuters.

Dr. Kostner became interested in virtual teams about ten years ago. She was a team member on a high performance multi-site, multi-functional, multi-company project team. Despite the thousands of miles that split team members, geography was not a barrier. The virtual team successfully launched a product that still marks its success.

That project team launched her into writing five books for Houghton Mifflin and Glencoe/Macmillan/ McGraw Hill. It also gave her a key focus for her doctoral degree in communication at the University of Denver, where she earned her Ph.D. in 1990. Dr. Kostner is a professional speaker, writer, and author whose client list includes some of the most progressive companies in the world.